Poetry from the Depths
The Journey of a Wandering Soul

Sergio Felix Nicene

Radical Dream Books—Madison, WI
ISBN: 979-8-218-41046-9
Library of Congress Control Number: 2024911811
Title: *Poetry from the Depths: The Journey of a Wandering Soul*
Author: Sergio Felix Nicene
Digital distribution | 2024
Paperback | 2024

Dedication

iii

To my future wife and supportive family

Forgiveness to the Uttermost

Why am I here, on this Earth?
Is there anyone who thinks I have any worth?
I fight and I struggle within,
Barely hanging on to my closest kin.
My mind is a force for wrong,
And my heart will wax evil afore long.
I cry out to my Master, the Creator,
In hopes He will heal me later.
My family may be a reason to live,
But there is only one man, my heart will I give:
I look to the one and only Lamb,
In hopes of a slight blessing of mercy.
I sin over and over again in my flesh,
Fighting my demons, who seem not to rest,
Just when I think a new victory has come
I fall into temptation, the devil has won,
I look to the sky; my heart melted in sorrow,
My evil it reeks, deep into the marrow.
But lo, there is good news to behold,
The Master, the Creator of all,
Will forgive us our sins, no matter how tall.

Fudgecutter

Twas the day after Christmas,
The household was eager
To mayhap catch a glimpse
Of a man so meager

What's more exciting than Christmas?
Some people may ask.
I will tell you the truth
Tis a very hard task

Maybe if you saw him
You might even say,
The fudge cutters real
I saw him today

They lay out their fudge
Every elder every young
Both boy and girl
To stick on their tongue

A morsel bit size;
Many endless supplies
An uplifting snack
That you can't take back

What name does he go by?
What prize does he seek?
The fudge cutter's his name
He's out to seek the meek

Yet it's all just a guise
An uplifting surprise
The fudge cutter's there

To spread Christmas cheer

So come one come all
To this marvelous fest
Glittered with joy
And taste the best

As he leaves behind charity
He asks you favorable
Remember those before you
Honor what they do
Send a message and letter
To make their season better

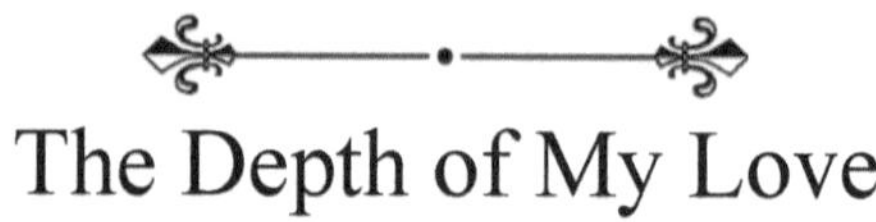

The Depth of My Love

If my love
Were measured in diamonds
No one else would own one
Because no one's love compares to mine

If my love
Were measured in water
There wouldn't be any left
Because I drown it all out with my love

If my love
Were measured in pain
I'd be a martyr for you
To show you I'd give everything
So you would know my eternal love

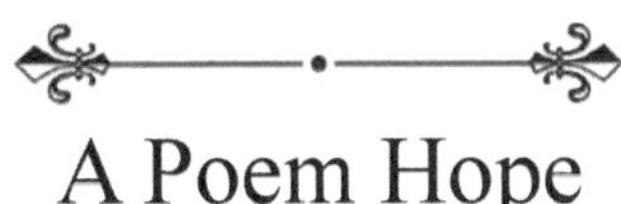

A Poem Hope

I once was bound in despair
Until I heard news through the air
The news of one who came to save
I searched my head and left my cave

For in my cave there was no hope
Just thought and demons forbidding me to cope
But all that changed upon a cross
When one man's life took away all loss

Once cursed as I looked above
Swearing I would never come to love
Not people no way no how
Not my creator of whom I now bow

Now I look forward eyes full of light
Saved from sorrow I reach a new height
What have I found that I hold so dear?
Why it is hope for my savior is near

The Legacy of a Generation

My passion, my home, my nation
Once founded by a righteous generation
darkened with many a blemished sensation
The land of the free and just; now in lamentation

Yet rooted in liberty hope and Godliness
Where one can voice his say with hardiness
Still my place of haven and refuge
Or to go where ones hearts lead in news

Still a lingering hope preserves
Dressed as angels we get our deserves
Though brutal attacks fool many
Straying from our God uncanny

Yet lost causes are worth fighting for
Our ancestor's posterity must fight more
Our visions, dreams, and hopes are eternal
While writing of peace in our never-ending journal

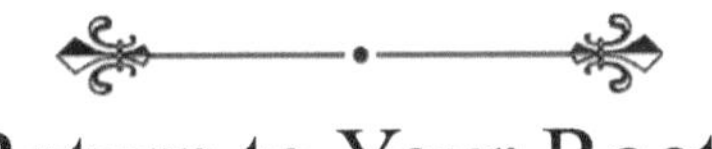

Return to Your Roots

Return America to the root of Freedom!
Don't leave their beliefs and words decaying in a museum
Remember your fathers and reclaim their spirit
Listen to their words: you need to rehear it

Evil doers twist lies and confuse the truth
The dark hour reveals their bloodthirsty tooth
But we must not feel shaken
The Word says we are never forsaken

Mayhap the people will unite under God
Think these trials rather odd?
And learn to stand for truth once more
These are the trials that allow us to soar!

Learning to stand for justice again
The light from above shines like it's been
We rise above that city on a hill
Radiating more gloriously than any mans will

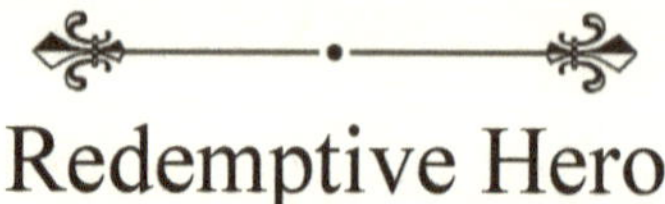

Redemptive Hero

A dark knight is reborn
His racing mind looks back at his past in scorn
Overwhelmed with his dark past of forlorn
Fighting for justice he has now sworn

He is filled with grief and sorrow
Looking everywhere for inner peace to borrow
He is haunted by those memories to the marrow
Becoming a light for the worlds tomorrow

No more does he desire the dark
He painstakingly searches for that spark
To roam free from his sin
Is the only way for him to win

He walks with newfound purpose
He starts a new path on a new surface
Abiding with purity and light
Mercy compassion makes him bright

Avenging the just and pure of heart
He aims to fill a higher chart
Once filled with darkness and wrath
He has turned to a righteous path

Now a soldier of the light
He fights for justice of souls without might
Always protecting the weak
Now at peace he fights for those meek

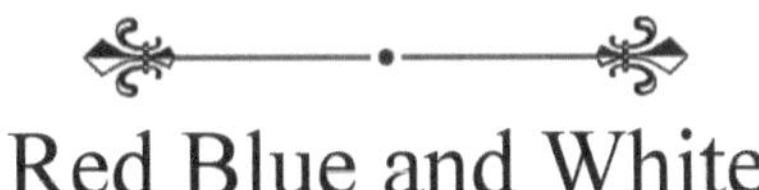

Red Blue and White

Red for valor
Bravely enlisting
Fearlessly fighting
With the red blood
Soiling the ground
For freedom

Blue for vigilance
Never ceasing watch
Standing strong relentlessly
Sailing the blue
Both sky and sea
For justice

White for purity
Never seeking war
Always bidding peace
Among the brotherhood
Of Adams race
For our prosperity

They Live!!

Unborn child
You'll have pain
But witness marvels
Exciting that precious mind

Unborn child
You'll get bored at times
But exciting thrills await
Taking you places unforgettable

Unborn child
Sorrow is necessary
To fully get joy
Balance will complete you

Unborn child
You'll see loss
But you'll experience wonders
That will never leave you

Unborn child
If no one wants you
God will take you in as His own child
Protecting you from all ails

Unborn child
You will be loved
Always by your Creator
Watching over in tender mercy

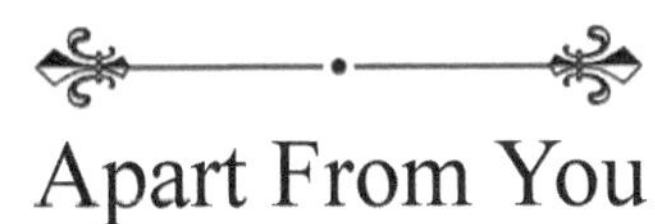

Apart From You

Apart from you
I'm vain and conceited
With no one but myself
To care for

Apart from you
I search my innermost depths
And see darkness and pain
My lifeblood depleting hourly

Apart from you
I love with reservation
Patiently waiting for you
To make life worthwhile

But with you
I have someone
To love and cherish
Who reciprocates it
Making me whole

But with you
My pain is washed away
Filled with joy from you
Springing eternally
Binding us closer

And with you
My love has no limit
For your heart is boundless
Able to receive endless charity

Alone

Alone
There I was…
Alone
Surrounded by the masses…
Rejected
Looking for someone…
Anyone
Crying for help…
Anywhere
Hoping for someone…
To save me
Try to stay steady…
To stay strong
Listening to the voices…
Gibberish
Mind going everywhere…
Racing
Finding an ally…
A true brother

Rejected

We get rejected
We get abused
We get shafted
We get left behind
We get forgotten

We rise above
We rise with love
We rise over trials
We rise in hope
We rise for goodwill

We hope in truth
We hope in purity
We hope with charity
We hope in goodness
We hope to end strife

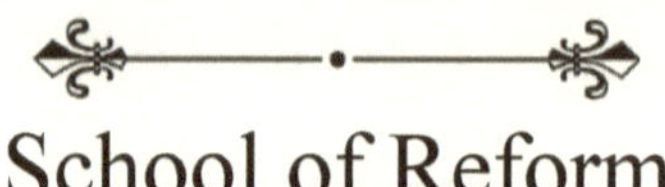

School of Reform

Why do the heathen rage?
Why do the foolish seek war?
Why do the vain seek self-glory?
Why do the warmongers spread fear?
Why do the criminals attack innocent?

They rage for glory
They seek war for filthy lucre
They seek glory for selfish pride
They spread fear for power
They attack for gain

How do we prevent rage?
How do we stop money obsessing?
How do we end selfish pride?
How do we cease the lust for power?
How do we stop selfish gain?

By showing the benefits of peace
By explaining the meaning of life
By exhorting the value of others
By giving it to the people
By showing the value of charity

Sacrifice

Our hero lay defeated
Our hero lay alone
Our hero lay crushed
Our hero lay lost

The darkness was present
The losses were never ceasing
The hope was being lost
The dreams were dashed to pieces

Yet strength had not ceased
Yet fortitude was present
Yet courage remained
Yet faith was still a whisper

Instead of hiding… He found hope
Instead of crying… He rose valiantly
Instead of laying low… He faced his destiny
Instead of fearing… He risked his life for all

Hidden Beauty

Her beauty is Hidden
Her eyes are full of compassion
Her ears listen in kindness
Her mouth speaks charity
Her hands give the gift of warmth
Her breathing proves her modesty
Her walk shows her purity
Her talks value others
Her hug grants great comfort
Her legs walk good tidings around
Her heart is filled with joy
Her hair exposes her freedom
Her beliefs solidify her sainthood
Her love changes people's hearts
Her conversation converts people to truth
Her loyalty lasts forever
Her testimony is eternal

New Beginnings

I ran swiftly
Not knowing where
Not looking back
No guilt no shame
Only seeking to begin anew

I thought quietly
At the memories
At the pressures
At the failures
Happy to leave it behind

I found hope anew
Happy to find work
Happy to find friends
Happy to find a home
Ready to begin anew

The Earth and All of its Fullness

Days glow afresh
Shining forth
In glorious light
Going forward
To blaze trials anew

Mountain overlooks
Rivers shimmer
Woodlands sing
Canyons echo
Land was made for you

Eternity glistens
Nature screams
Times stops
Earth is yours
Forever

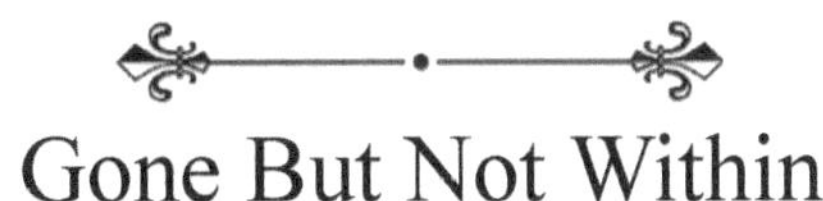

Gone But Not Within

They're gone
But not within
We remember
We recall
We never forget

Their memories shine
Their face glistens
Their voice echoes
Their wisdom endures
Their love remains

Irreplaceable
Unforgettable
Stuck forever as memories of light
Timeless in my time
They remain within my heart

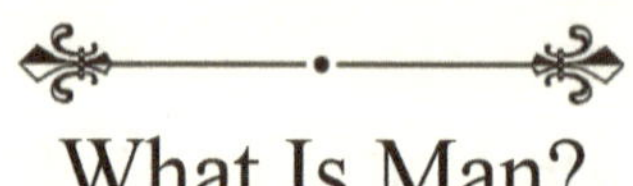

What Is Man?

Man is deeper than meets the eye
Man is funnier than imagination can create
Man is wiser than time flies
Man its weirder than animals can imitate
Man Is heart-filled more than the mind thinks

Man is greedier than a bank
Man is as jealous as an ex
Man is sadder than the tears of heaven
Man is goofier than cotton candy
Man is more helpless than a lost dog

Man is as redeemable as credit
Man is as hopeful as a new day
Mans is as precious as a newborn
Man is as worthwhile as life
Man is unforgettable as we stand the test of time

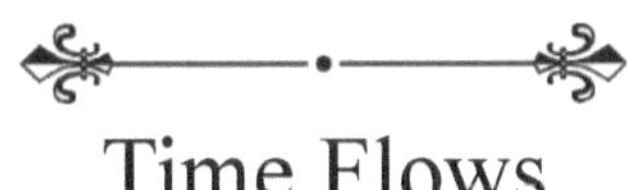

Time Flows

On all fours we crawl
Speaking each language in gibberish
Seeing our surroundings our eyes open
Hearing the sounds of life in awe
In the arms of safety blissful

On two feet we run for freedom
Speaking one language we socialize
Seeing the world, we gaze in wonder
Hearing our favorite music enthralled
Figuring out the way of life

On a cane we creep forward
Speaking in riddles and wisdom
Seeing the world as it was
Hearing the cries of past loved ones
Reminiscing yesteryear as we await our fate

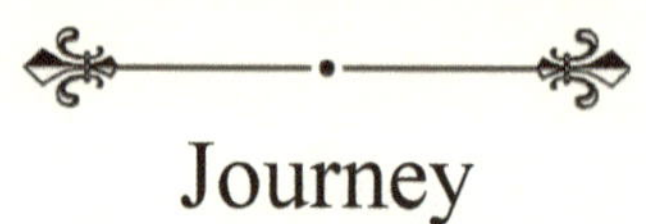

Journey

Broke down
We weep

Head strong
We fall

Marching forward
We stumble

Looking for answers
We're lost

Strengthened within
We laugh

Built up
We rise

Blazing paths
Others follow

Answering questions
Purpose is found

Dreams

Of peace within
Of harmony amongst friends
Of the unity of allies
Of charity to the poor
Of goodwill to neighbors
Of bonding within families
Of trust amongst partners
Of selflessness towards others
Of hatred of lucre
Of distance from welfare
Of hope for the future
Of innovation that excites
Of science that discovers
Of religion that purifies
Of life that preservers
Of dreams that endure

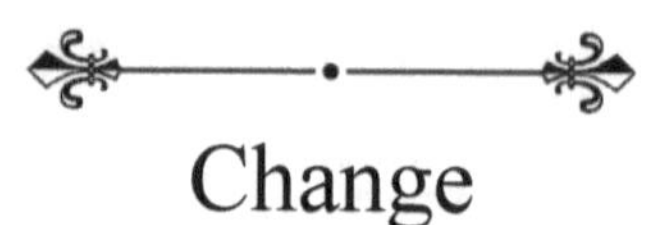

Change

I was…
Weak
Foolish
Fragile
Weeping
Conceited
Selfish

I am…
Strengthened
Wisened
Fortified
Compassionate
Humbled
Selfless

I will…
Overcome
Enlighten
Carry on
Befriend
Be gracious
Sacrifice

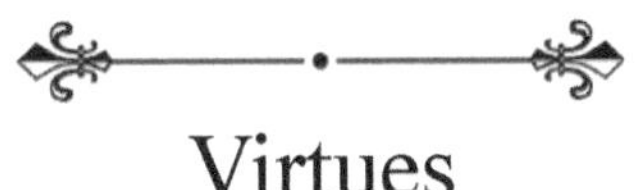

Virtues

S tay strong…
With mercy

Stay wise…
With humility

Stay brave…
with compassion

Stay honest…
with goodwill

Stay righteous…
with sincerity

Stay fortified…
with meekness

Stay holy…
with purity

Stay lowly…
with dignity

Stay peaceful…
with justice

Stay thankful….
with understanding

Stay hungry…
with a love of life

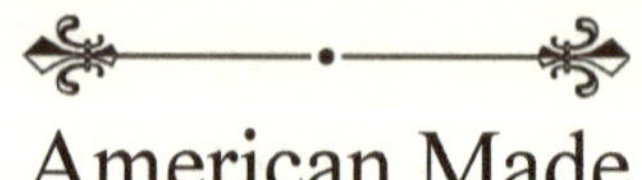

American Made

Child of the republic…
  Be strong like the mountain
  Unmovable in your resolve
Unchangeable in your ways of virtue
Impenetrable in your fortitude

Child of the free...
Be wise as the wind
Always searching yet never satisfied
Helpful to strangers yet steady to kin
Going where your heart deems worthy

Child of the brave...
Be courageous as the waterfall
Not afraid to make a leap of faith
Purifying your cells amongst the rocks
Showering the world with uncanny fearlessness

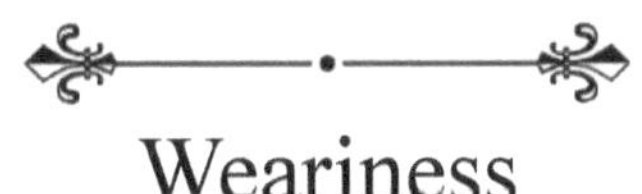

Weariness

Weary hands…
Continue to work despite the pain

Weary legs…
keep marching to the best of life

Weary eyes…
Fight those tears and see life

Weary mind…
don't quit chasing the answers

Weary tongue...
keep preaching the truth

Weary ears…
keep listening for peace

Weary heart…
never quit loving

Weary body…
ignore the pain and thrive

Weary soul…
you fight, rest is for the dead

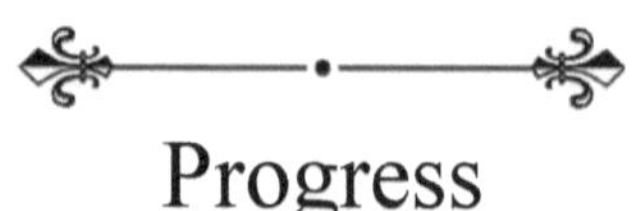

Progress

We love for unity
We unite for peace
We peace for progress
We progress for wonder
We wonder for creativity
We create to gaze
We gaze to seek
We seek to love
We love for unity
Forever

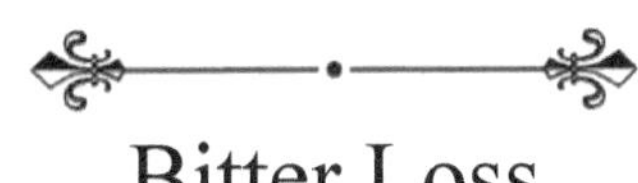

Bitter Loss

I cried… they mocked
I explained… they didn't understand
I showed… they rejected
I created… they destroyed

He ran… they followed
He spoke… they listened
He wept… they comforted
He invented... they appreciated

I reached out… he laughed
I pleaded… he punished
I desired peace… he already obtained
I wanted fellowship… He was engulfed in friends

He looked down… at me
He ripped up… my words
He terrorized… my hopes
He conquered… my people's hearts

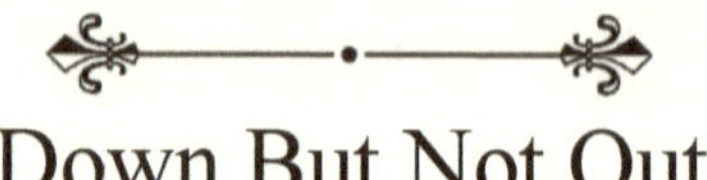

Down But Not Out

Broken-down, beaten, but not conceding
Lost and alone, but not friendless
Tired, in despair but not lifeless
Poor and in debt yet full of love
Terrorized, in danger but still brave
Brainwashed and indoctrinated yet still open
Weak and powerless but capable
Push and pulled but in one piece
Ripped and shredded but strengthened in heart
Mocked and scorned but smiling
Flattered and mislead but honest still
Attacked and accused but a steadfast reputation
Forgotten and left behind yet at peace within
Rejected by all but her, endless love

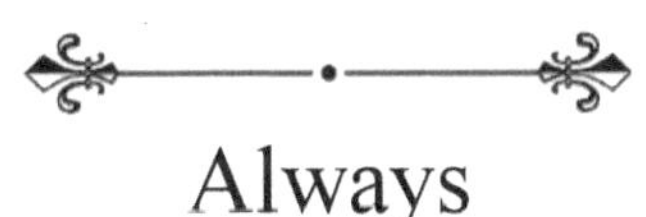

Always

If you're in pain
I will feel it
I will be beside you
I will aid your aliment
However, I can
Always

If you are lost
I will guide you
I will comfort you
I will make you forget the unknown
And show you
This is where you were meant to be
With me
Always

If you are lonely
Wherever you are
I'll be beside you
Guiding you
Loving you
Cherishing you
Supporting you
Always

If you're in sorrow
I'll wipe those tears
I'll cry for you
I'll take it upon myself
Until you laugh
And weep no more
Always

If you are poor
I will give you my love
I will show you laughter
I will make the rich envy you
For the all the love and good
That comes your way
Always

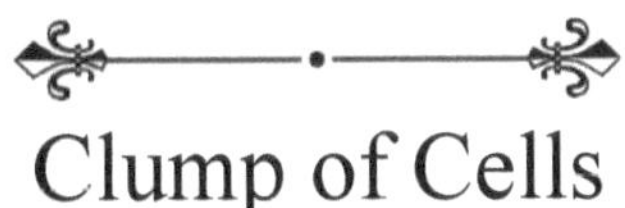

Clump of Cells

The clump of cells grew
The clump of cells had feet and hands
The clump of cells could feel
The clump of cells fight with everything
The clump of cells came out a dead baby

The parasite was alive
It took energy from its host
The parasite had a heart like its mom!
The parasite wanted life
The parasite was just a dead baby when it came out

The unwanted baby smiled
The unwanted baby had eyes like her mom
The unwanted baby had the most adorable smile
The unwanted baby loved its mom- it knew who gave her nutrients
But the unwanted baby was unwanted so it was just a dead baby when
it came out

I Cried for My Sins

I cried for my sins
I hated myself for my transgressions
I was on the verge of ending it all
Because the vilest men could condemn me justly
Could I be forgiven… for the worst of thoughts?

It all seemed like a big lie
Like a big fantasy
Why did God wanna redeem me?
How could He? I was His villain
A monster He created like Lucifer
what is the point of me
wandering in the time space

I used to believe in God
Love cherish and walk with Him
But what now? what do you call a severed friendship
Are we enemies now?
I deserve hellfire

Yet God had mercy on me
He said... I have not forgotten you
I would rather have a sinner
An honest wretched sinner come
And degrade themselves
Than a sinless man boast

But will we ever be close like we once were?
Will I ever find solace in your presence
That carried me my first 30 years?
What good am I Lord?
Was I created to suffer and nothing else?
Do I have a woman out there? or is that an illusion

A hook to fool me and find unbreathable air
Destined to face my loneliness alone

When will you come back to me oh Word of God??
I miss you more than I love her
Cause you always showed me you Loved me
And you always told me the pain it cost
To redeem my wretched soul…
Was I worth it Christ????
Was I worth that pain…
What is my value to you Great Creator??
Forgive me for my pride Lord

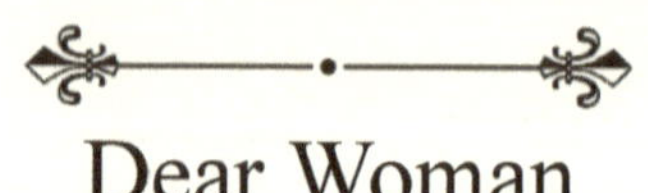

Dear Woman

Dear woman:
Do you still love me?
Despite my shortcomings
After I've revealed it all

Do you still trust me?
Do you still want me
Despite knowing the worst of me?
Do you trust me to stay loyal to you?

Do you think I'd be a good father?
A good husband?
A good man?

Are you still crazy about me?
Or has your passion wavered?
I'm trying my best to stay true
To God
To the Bible
To Jesus

But I'm a conflicted confused man
Obsessed with you
Please don't give up on me
I
Love
You
Still

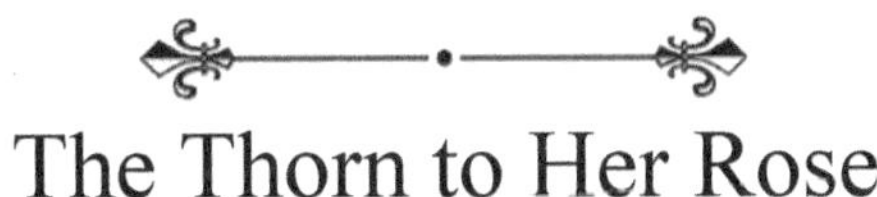

The Thorn to Her Rose

I wait patiently for my love
I dream of her character
Because I need her holiness
So, I can stay true

I wait eagerly for my lover
I ponder her personality
Hoping it matches mine
So, every line is harmony

I fervently desire to see her
Those angelic looks on earth
Why waste such beauty on me?
Yet my eyes shall be in awe

As time passes my desire grows for her
When I meet her can I be disappointed?
Her soul shines forth in each action of beauty
Her whole being was made to reflect glory from the sun
And I was made to complete her: the thorns to her rose

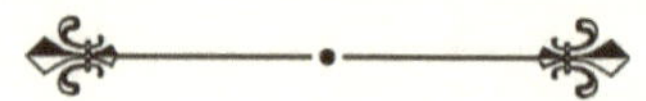

We Were Made Together Like Nature

We are hydrogen and oxygen
Creating fluid while in harmony
Flowing together through time
Becoming inseparable as one

We are the cold autumn days
Our past falling as leaves
Our future being tested by harsh cold
Yet even in the white of winter we shine brilliantly

We are the baby blue sky
Water in white puffs of imagination
Surrounded by serene celestial blue
Covering the sky with our love

We are the soil of regeneration
Nutrients keeping us youthful as we age
Of dust we came and of dust we leave
Yet ours shall leave a soil in the hearts of future generations

Water the Essence of Life

As water flows till it reaches its destination
Finally finding where it belongs in peace
So, my love flows forward until you come into my life
Searching for meaning until it can rest

As rain falls strengthening the earth
Giving nutrients to soil and energy to life
So, to do my words pour out on you
Hoping to shine forth as wisdom

As waterfalls create energy
For making humans transcend
So, to do I hope my desires for a better world
Reach the hearts and minds to make change

As wind transforms water
Into a devastating tsunami
So, I hope my hatred of wickedness
Destroys the seeds of evil sown in some hearts

Imagine the Depth of Our Love

If I loved you this much
Without knowing a lick about you
Imagine the love ill have
When I meet you and discovery
All you have to offer

If I care about you this much
Without knowing you
Imagine how much ill care
When I develop a deep bond
Where your depth of soul reaches mine

If I want you this badly now
Imagine how intense my desire for you
Will consume me as I see your beauty
Both internally and the externally
I'll see that and lose my mind again
In a tranquil ecstasy all of my life

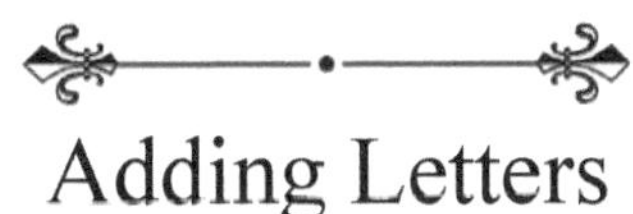

Adding Letters

I waited to get better
And suffered for it
Nothing made sense in those days
Different parts of my being weren't together

My mind wasn't plugged in right
My spirit couldn't tell wrong from wrong
And my emotions felt pain and forgot pleasure
I had trouble formulating logic

A plus b did not equal c
But when was that ever true
Yet my mind keeping seeking
What a plus b equaled

Searching fervently in earnest
Finally deciding letters were too complex to add
So, I tried words instead

Never Give Up on Lost Causes

My spirit lost its faith in a higher power
I was left at a cave with nothing
Nothing to believe in nothing to hope for
So, my soul drifted about seeking
Something somewhere to help me
And lo and behold my greatest enemy

He who hated good was the only one that cared
My emotions were everywhere
Everywhere except up
They were down sideways and spinning
Never knowing how to steady
As I raged at peace
And confused friendship with strife

They made me feel alone
Gradually I was restored
But I still couldn't rationalize
I still had not faith
I still felt emotions of boredom and loneliness
So, I continued down the path of pain
Clueless as ever
Yet with a dash of hope

That hope was enough
Enough for my endurance
And my sanity came back
My God had not forsaken me...
Evil was wrong again
And I restored from beast to man

Possibilities

What if I lose you?
After all the pain
All the effort
All the searching
What if it's all for naught?

If you and I are no longer we
What if I become a different man?
Grow cold
Grow tired
Grow grumpy and obscene
What if I hate what I become
But have no ability to change?

What if I'm not what you signed up for?
All the promises of poetry
The smoothness of words
The highest ideologies
What If that's not me
And you see the real empty shallow man I am?

What if my love isn't enough?
What if I keep my promises
What if my poetry rhymes to the soul
What if it gets repetitious
What if you need more than I can offer?
For I am a monster in flesh compared to your beauty
And maybe you need a better man

What if it isn't the will of God?
What if He want us to suffer?
He created us to be apart
He wanted us to be an example

Of how not to fall for lust
How to put God first

Is this a test Almighty?
Will you have mercy
And let me and her be we?

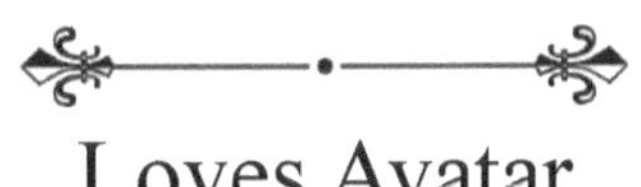

Loves Avatar

My love,
If my mind could feel,
It would feel love for your you

My love,
If my heart could speak,
It would sing of your virtues

My love,
If my hands could experience your brilliance,
They be enlightened like the renaissance

My love,
If my voice could see you
It would marvel at your pure beauty

My love,
If my love for you could talk,
The language would be divine angel speak

My love,
If time could contain my emotions,
It would erupt like a volcano of the purest love

For my love for you
Is a Holy love
Begun in Christ
Lasting eternal
Wiling to suffer
Pulling you up when your down
And always cherish you no matter the trial
My love strengthens with each hardship I encounter
The more I feel pain the more I can love you

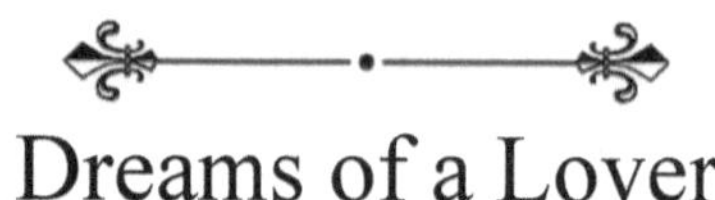

Dreams of a Lover

I think of my dream of her
The love
The sacrifice
The passion

But what does she dream of?
What is her love she desires
What is the sacrifice she has to make?
What is the passion she wants?
What makes her tick?

I think of my hopes for the future
My goals
My dreams
Our shared connections

But what about her?
What are her goals
What are her dreams
What does she share or not wanna share?
What is in her heart?

As a man
I desire her
For everything
To be my forever
To be my best friend
My submissive partner that often has superiority
To share my beliefs, my God

But as a woman…
What are her desires
If me, why?

If me, how can I keep it that way eternally?
Does she want everlasting love
Is she that committed
Does she want me to be her everything
Or is she truly too good for me to handle

Does she want me to be her best friend?
What does she want in me?
Can we share the same beliefs goals and God
Or is that impossible?

Can be truly be united?
Or are we destined for troubled waters?
Can we be each other's answer?
Or are we too complex?

Can we have a hierarchy
With her submitting to me?
Or is she superior?
Can we truly be one…
Or was that a fallacy from the start?
But
What if it works out?

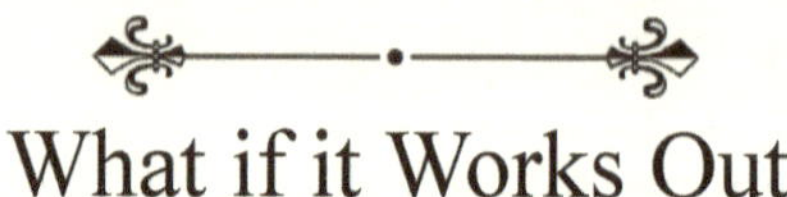

What if it Works Out

What if it works out
I wondered
What if I lost her love
That I faded in obscenity
Into anger bitterness or boringness
Consumed the both of us

But then again what if it works out?
What if we never lose our love
That we stay in healthy passion
Into peace betterment and excitement
Engulf both of us forever
What if we never lose our love?

I wondered what If I couldn't be there for her?
What if I became a crippled; a crutch
That I lose my health to be able to take of her
Couldn't lover her or meet her needs
As she met my needs instead?

But then again what if it works out?
What If we both stay healthy?
What if were both there for each other
Always
That we both pull our fair share
Sacrifices and jobs endeavored
What if we both live good long healthy lives?

I wondered if we could follow God still
What if God was angry?
Or didn't want us together?
That we went against the Almighty's will?
Would we get to have a forever?

But what if it was Gods will?
What if God was pleased
And had been waiting for us to be together?
That we were the will of the Father
Forever?

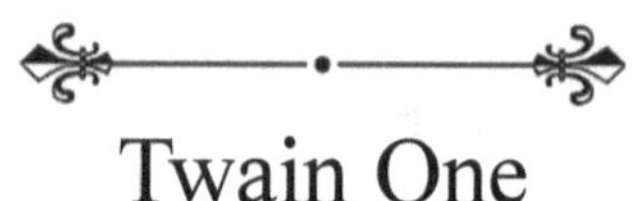

Twain One

The one and only
The tireless dreamer
The wanter of one

I dreamed of another
A matched dream
The wanter of one

Twain becomes one
Together we dream
United we are one

We Always Have a Choice

We always have a choice
When we lose, we lose with class
When we fall, we learn how to pick ourselves up
When we are offended, we forgive with grace
When we falter, we do so with dignity
When we leave, we go away quietly
When we win, we win with compassion
When we rule, we rule with mercy
When we are the victim, we fight with truth
When we exit a scuffle, we do so peacefully
When we fight a war, we do so with just cause
When we lie, we set things straight
When we are questioned, we answer honestly
When we fight, we respect our opponent
When schism arises amongst brothers, we seek unity
When difficulties arise, we grow stronger
When we are afraid, we pray harder
When our beliefs are challenged, we seek the truth
When hypocrites amass, we expose them
When the bad guys win, we don't give up
When times get tough, we keep grinding
When the world seems like it is dying, we set seeds of hope and truth
When we live, we do so with elan
When are children ask, we teach wisdom
When it's between death or selling out we die a noble death
When the world goes mad, we stand our ground
When it's a lost cause we fight harder
When our live is over we left it a better place

How Can There Be Logic Without Understanding?

How can we ask… without knowledge
How can we seek… without direction
How can we stand… without strength
How can we discover… without curiosity
How can we debate… without facts
How can there be good… without evil
How can there be choice… without free will
How can there be hypocrisy… without truth
How can there be joy… without sorrow
How can we condemn… when we have done worse
How can we unify…if there aren't differences
How can we fight… without violence
How can we comprehend… without a higher power
How can we have a family…without a home
How can you sacrifice…. without passion
How can you suffer for another… without calling them brother
How can we forsake… when we can help
How can there be life… without death
How can there be peace… without laws
How can there be inner peace… without a struggle
How can there be free will… without the ability to do wrong
How can there be forgiveness… without transgression
How can there be redemption… without a fall
How can we love… unless we were first loved
how can we trust…. without proof
How can we betray… without dissenters
How can we blossom… without time
How can we love… without another
How can we experience… without life
How can there be artist… without critics
How can we philosophize…without discerners

How can we create… without creation
How can there be a just God… without judgment
How can there be mercy... without a way out
How can there be a soul… without immortality
How can there be depth… without a Deeper Supreme Being

Without Imperfection…What Do We Aspire To?

At the end of eternity…
Lies the end of pain
Lies the end of sorrow
Lies the end of lies
Lies the end of hypocrisy
Lies the end of strife
Lies the end of forgetting everything that stung the heart

At the end of forever …
Begins the lost dreams
Begins the broken promises
Begins the lost causes
Begins the broken relationships
Begins the lost discoveries
Begins the start of a new age of nothing with a new ideal of hope

At the end of the never-ending…
What gets carried over?
What will last?
Will there be time?
How do we start over?
When we learn virtue?
And carry forth the sword of peace?
What will stop us from repeating the nightmares of the last ending?

The Meaning of Weaknesses

Sorrow just means you have compassion
Nervousness means you wanna do well
Fear shows you respect power
Pain show you have strength to conquer it
Tears show that you have care
Failure shows you tried
Teasing means your showing attention
Loss means you had
Being bullied gives you more to overcome
Hatred of evil means you disagree with evil
Challenge leads to a journey
Hard times strengthen you
Shyness means you care what people think
Being timid just means you are a dissector of yourself
Curiosity means you are seeking
Hopelessness is just a phase: can become hope with time
Being scared means you respect your opponent
Fear pushes us to go farther
Weakness just means we can improve
Being alone means we have room for friends
Bucking the trend makes us trailblazers
Standing alone leads to immortality

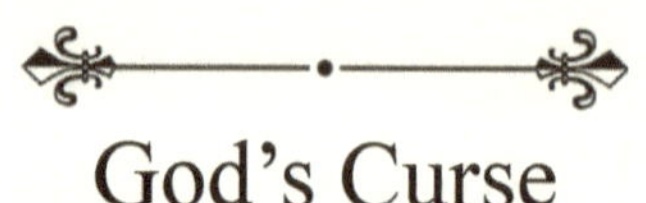

God's Curse

A hundred years ago
We lost ourselves
A people self-polluted
Our morals sank
We left God for pleasure
And God cursed us

Ninety years ago
We lost what was right
We made woman as corrupt as man
We penalized people for working
We created a league of villains
We esteemed us smarter than our fathers
And God cursed us

Eighty years ago
We lost our bread basket
The stock market crashed
We fight against the good guy
We welcomed the Jew
We gave up on liberty
And God cursed us

Today we live in hell
Gay flags can't be burnt but Americas can
Kids are taught sex in primary school
Woman are told motherhood is beneath them
Men and women live like whores and manwhores
The only race that's racist are the whites
Whites are almost a minority

Murdering a baby is a right
The working man is taxed beyond his weight

Welfare is commonplace
Politicians are puppets for whoever pays the most
Every industry is fifth- LGBTQ is the tip of the iceberg
We don't have freedom of speech

They strip our rights daily
White people get killed and no one bats an eye
Every race is proud of their race- except whites
And the ultimate sin is to be anti jew
But can you imagine what it would look like without Jews?
Or minorities, what a paradise
Will God allow us to survive?
Or is this His final curse?

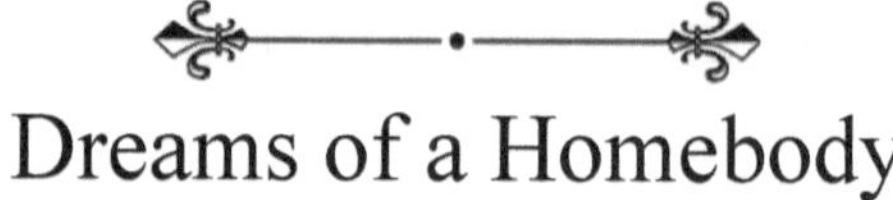

Dreams of a Homebody

My dream
Is to see you smile
Forgetting all your troubles
Replaced by us together
Through all life trials

My hope
Is to make you happy
Letting you experience
The joys of life
With me by your side

My desire
Is to watch you mother our kids
Who learn from you
The ways of truth
And shine forth as lights

My wants
Are seeing you shine for me
Radiating as the stars
For no one else but me
Making my dreams reality

My passion
Is seeing the best of you
Doing every bit my part
To make your life worthwhile
And your trials redeemable

My fulfillment
Is only possible with you
As two become one

One is crippled without its half
But perfected with its missing part

My name,
Is to be one with you
Sharing life's struggles
And enjoying life's joys
Together with our brood

My rest,
Will be next to you set in stone
For the ages to see
And awake together at the trumpet
With our Lord in paradise together

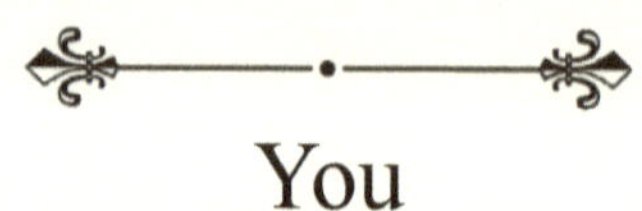

You

I searched for you
Not knowing
Your virtues
Your radiant cheer
Blindly I look
Hoping against odds
That you exist
That you won't let my burning heart fail
Will I ever see you?
Your smile of cheer
Your strength of comfort
Your eyes that shine
As the stars of the sea
Radiating all life…
When will I be we??

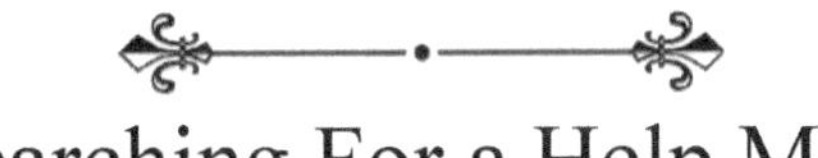

Searching For a Help Mate

I walked alone
With no one but my Savior
Searching for you
Praying for you
Begging for you
But He said wait
You're not ready
I lost Him
Or so I thought

So, I had nothing
And I lost my faith
So, I searched for you
The next best thing
But you never came
I prayed till you became an idol
All I cared about was you
Finding you
Being near you
Knowing you

But I knew about as much about you
As I did an unwritten fantasy
I wanted so much from you
I requested you be virtuous and kind
I desired intelligence and understanding
I sought for you to have the best personality

I wanted you to be the greatest Christian
To love God more than me
And I wanted pure beauty that all would stand in awe
I poured out my soul by writing you passionately
I wrote as if you could read

I spoke as If I knew you

I searched as Adam did throughout the garden
But I received nothing
So, God took me back and said,
"Your prayers are never in vain
I've planned for you two since before the dawn of Creation"
And I said, "Lord be our God Forever
And let her know how greatly she is loved.

"Don't let her ever spend a day without knowing
That she is loved above all women of the world by me
Protect her always above me
And tell her she shall never walk alone"

Your Name is Eden

When we meet
All my worries will be put to rest
I'll hear the words of grace
I'll witness your steadfast love to the truth
All my tests you'll pass with ease
You'll show me things I never new
And welcome me into a world of wonder

When we meet
I can't be let down
Because I have to have a better half!
There must be equilibrium
A soul that compliments mine!
That takes what I have
And transcends us to new heights!!
For what worth is man without woman?
And what good is greatness without a complimentary wonder?

When we meet
I wanna tell you how much I love you from the start
All the tears I've cried trying to stay pure for you
All the struggles I've fought looking for you
But first I want know everything about you
I want you to be my muse
My lifelong search for deeper love and purer passion
My reason for challenging the demons and conquer them

When we meet
I want it to last forever
To replace Romeo and Juliet as the love story
To take place on this earth and leave decedents forever
A family of character and righteousness
Going on till the end of the world

While we worship the sun
Together in paradise

Without You

Without you, my life is shallow
If I were a great intellectual
And wrote books on philosophy
Revolutionizing our way of thought
I'd still feel worthless without you my dear

If I was the greatest scientist
Transforming fields with new discoveries
Saving millions of lives
The accomplishments would mean little without you my love

If I was a once in a generation statesman
That saved America from threats domestic and foreign
That united the people and ushered a new era of freedom
I'd still feel shallow and alone without you my soul mate

For what good is philosophy with love?
And what worth is science without compassion?
And what purpose does a country have without families?
But you are my greatest discovery,
And winning your heart will be my greatest achievement

If I Could Just Give You a Good Life, My Life Would Be Bliss

If I were a plumber
Working in cruddy situations
Getting dirty and gritty
But if I still had you
And could somehow provide for you
I'd consider myself the luckiest man alive

If I were a middle school teacher
And had to put up with annoying kids daily
They're whining their adolescence immaturity and all
But I still had you
And could magically provide for you
I'd be excited to come home as the best part of my life daily

If I worked two jobs to keep our family afloat
It'd be tiring and exhausting
But seeing you at home with joy for the kids
With that love you have for your brood
I'd find a way to be strong and finally feel like I had a purpose
And your love for me would transform the pain to bliss

Idolatry

He showed me power
I said I don't care
He promised me a way out
I said I already have Jesus
He told me God was sinful
I said that's impossible
He told me of he could give me anything
I said I don't trust you
He showed me unlimited power
I said I'd rather have love
So, he said I have the perfect girl
I asked if she was a Christian
He said she was perfect
I said I'd already been praying for her so God will provide
He was quiet…
So, I thought I'd won
But I loved her more, more than Jesus
I have no idea how or why
All my life id prayed
"Help me to love you more than anything
Future wife and future children included"
But somehow, when I was weak
All I thought of was her
She was a fantasy, a dream
But I loved her more than Jesus
So, I wasn't worthy
The devil had won
Can I get back to loving the Creator??
Or am I destined to fall into fire forever????
Lord have mercy on my soul…

Why Do You Torment Me Woman!!

I never met her
But I knew she was there
From the pain
The tormenting suffering I endured!!!
The pain of her not around consumed me
I tried to forget
But I knew she was out there

I tried to let go
But I never had her
So the pain stayed
The pain permeated
Spread from by heart to my mind
Nay the whole body was in pain
From missing my core

The pain engulfed me
I knew it was a sin
Loving one more than God
And I hated myself
But I loved her so much
And it wouldn't leave

I don't need to know the details
I knew she was perfect for me
Cause I sent out a call for love
And only she truly got it
As there is only one God
I have only one lover…
Forever
Dear woman
Dearest woman
The one that hurts me just by being away

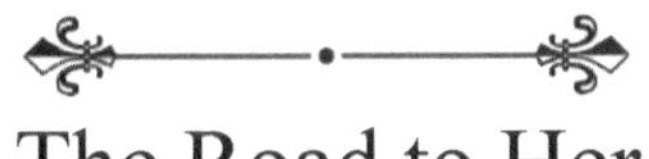

The Road to Her

It was you
That all those crushes led to
The nerves the butterflies
I never got lucky
But that's cause I am lucky
To have you

It was you
The one I prayed for daily
Who I begged and pleaded for
Higher and higher expectations
With each prayer
Yet you won't let me down

It was you
The one I was in pain for
Because you meant so much to me
I lost my desire for just anyone
And replaced it with you
Forever only you

It was you
The one that was made for me
The one that compliments me
That completes me
That gives me life
And loves me in equilibrium

Psy Ops

They took away our freedoms
One by one
We elected people to protect our freedoms
They did nothing
Their evil genius ideas consumed them
They wanted total control
A new age of man
Where they electronically control us
The new world order is upon us
It was never about gays
It was about destroying the family
It was never about women
It was about turning them against men
It was never about protecting women
It was about killing their offspring
It was never about the stopping gun violence
It was about Total control and no way to fight back
It was never about blacks
It was using them as a pawn
It was never about racism
It was about control over the one race that is always racist and can
never be proud of their heritage
It was never about diversity
It was about division
It was never about helping immigrants
It was about white genocide
It was never about a better life for them
It was about a worse life for you
It was never about education
It was about indoctrination
It's not about religious freedoms
It's about attacking Christianity
It was never about wars for democracy

It was money laundering
It was never republicans vs democrats
It was one party rule; aristocracy
It was never about America
It was about the Jews

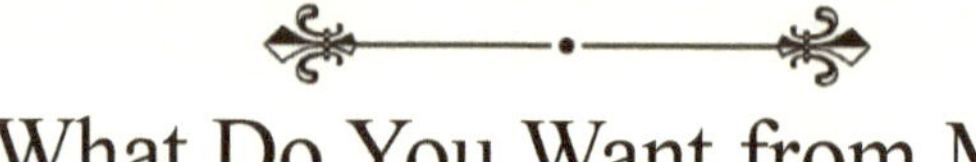

What Do You Want from Me??

I wrote to you
But you never replied
I prayed for you
But are you a believer?
I cried tears of pain
Because I felt like I let you down
But did you even care?

I waited an hour sitting at a diner
But you never showed.
I wanted to sacrifice for you
But we haven't even met…
I put up my signal for you
But where were you?
I wrote you almost daily
And I got not one word back

I tried to give up my addictions
To make you happy
Do you know how hard it gets?
I tried giving my life for yours
Because at least then one of us would be happy

Why does it sting so harshly
To be unknown
To be forgotten
To be invisible
By the one you love the most?

Why does the pain come
When I don't know you
When I can't be around you
When your nothing but a fantasy

Why can't you be real???
Why do they torment us?
Woman, do you love me?
How much?
Why?
Woman what do you see in me?

I see a waste
The epitome of pathetic
Your less than average failure
I don't even know if Jesus is the good guy!!!!
I just desperately want Him to be!!!

Forgive me
I'm the dung of the earth…
The slime ball of nature…
The poison rain of the world…

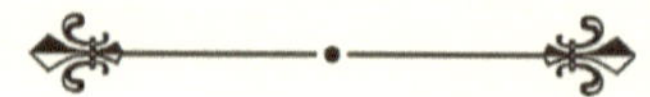

The Worth of Her Beautiful Soul

I asked for a few things personally….
But they held so much weight of gold
For you my dear one are worth more
More than all the possessions I'll ever own
More than my job career or all the money I'll make
More than the friendships ill accumulated
More than my own family to me
And outside of God my family the one thing I truly love deeply

I'm Sorry If I Made You Feel Terrible…

You're the stars in my night
The spring in my wilderness
The sunshine on my cloudy day
The cool breeze in my heat
The oasis in my desert
The rainbow on my rainy day
The pathway in my twisted forest
The island of peace in my ocean of chaos
The wildfire to restore my prairie
The tree vine to overcome my quicksand
My bridge over stormy water
The cave from dangerous weather
My eye of the hurricane with peace within
Where the whole world is falling apart
But we have perfect peace
Because we have each other

I'd Sacrifice for So Much More (You)

If I could become a slave for you to be free…
If I could take on pain for you to feel well….
If I could take on confusion for you to be at peace….
If I lost a part of me to make you feel whole…
If I had to walk alone for you to belong…
If I had to become impoverished for you to be rich….
If I had to lose myself for you to find yours…
If I had to lose my talents for you to find your gift….
If I had to hate for you to love
If I had to die for you to live
Then I could get it all back with your hand forever

Because you free me from inner slavery
Because you take away my pain
Because you give me such tremendous peace
Because you complete me
Because we are one together forever
Because your value is more than all precious metals combined
Because we suffer together and thrive as one
Because you are the greatest gift Jesus gave me
Because we balance each other out in perfect equilibrium
Because one's life is only as valuable as what he leaves behind

Quid Pro Quo

I'd give you my world
If I could get your time

I'd sacrifice my hours of free time
If I could converse with you

I'd give up my hobbies
If I could just go on walks with just you

I'd give up my most prized possessions
Just to hear that laugh and see that smile

I'd work extra hours
To see you happy at our home

I'd take the humiliation of romance
If I could show you daily my love

I'd put you in charge of all my money
Just to let you know your worth it and
That I trust you

I'd let you name one of our sons
But my names are too great;)
(Daughter tho;)

I'd give you my life
The joys the ecstasy
The pain when you're not there
O dear lover
How great is my love for you!!!
How do I prove it?
How do I let you know my love

And feel the way I do?
I'm thankful for you my deal

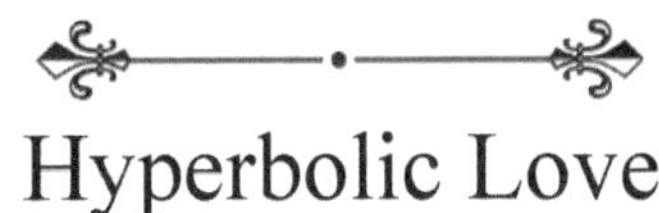

Hyperbolic Love

If my love for you were water
It would fill the entire ocean

If my love for you were a star
It would dwarf the sun

If my love for you were a road
It would never end

If my love for. you were precious metals
There wouldn't be any left to share

If my love for you were a book
It would be deep inspiring and life changing

If my love you for you were a word
It would mean love on steroids

If my love for you were a season
It would be constant and joyous

If my love for you were a river
It would be a wild ride of continuous bliss

If my love for you could be contained
I doubt the Milky Way would be large enough

If my love for you were a mountain
It would reach the heavens

If my love for you were power
It'd be as potent as a hurricane

If my love for you were sacrifice
I'd be willing to give up my world for your companionship forever

If my love for you were understanding
The whole world would know the meaning of romance

If my love for you were time
Everything would stop… as this is what creations been waiting for

Dream Girl... When Will We Meet?

I didn't know her
But I trusted her with my life
Blindly trusting in a higher power
To get us together
To keep her safe and true
To let her experience the love I have for her

I didn't know her
But I knew she had character
I knew she had virtue
And I knew of her beautiful soul
Because that's all I prayed for
Continuously without fail
And I trusted God would pull thru

I didn't know her
But I wanted her to have it all
I knew how great she wows
And didn't wanna let her down
I'm not much, personally I'm small
But I gots to be something more
So, I am worthy of her
And give her the life she deserves

I didn't know her
But my heart could feel hers
My soul told me she was real
My emotions went crazy about her
And logically I had to have a counterpart
So, I ran with my heart first
Eagerly waiting for her first appearance
So that I could always and forever
Know her…

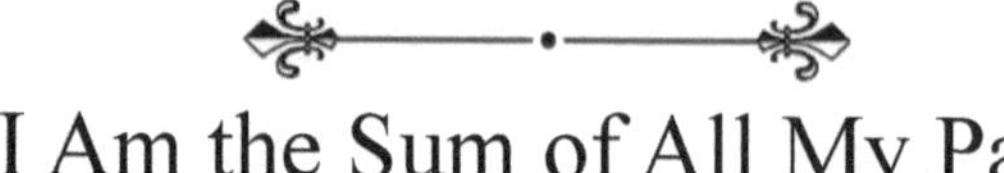

I Am the Sum of All My Pain

I am the pain from suffering
Mind body and soul
All tormented by weakness
Strengthening me

I am the disappointment of failure
Trying over and over
And getting nowhere
Making life more meaningful

I am the hurt of loss
My favorite people things ideas
All falling apart before my eyes
Making what I have more precious

I am the shortcomings of hope
Always wishing for the moon
But receiving a nightmare
Fire testing my faith to perfection

I am the sting of loneliness
Always seeking a friend
But walking the narrow path
Drawing closer to the Divine

I am the dashing of dreams
All my wants crushed by life
Stuck in a time loop of disappointment
Giving rise to my unbreakable spirit

I am the one who overcame
Bringing nothing into the world
Leaving my dreams and words of cheer
Regretting none of the hard times

Well It Doesn't Affect Me...

They paid us pennies for days of work
    But it wasn't enough

They taxed us on everything even imaginary crises
But it wants enough

They gave our money to everyone, except the sons
But that wants enough

They brought in the filth of world without measure
But it wasn't enough

We became a minority in our own land
But it wants enough

They forced debauchery of sexuality in everyway
But they kept pushing until pedophilia was legal
But it wasn't enough

They killed our unborn an made our women whores
But it wasn't enough

They made it illegal to speak out against them
Going after Christians who were anti-gay
But it wasn't enough

They lied about the global warming
Raising the taxes beyond measure
And damaging the environment
But it wasn't enough

They attacked anyone who said their name
And took away all their money and assets

But it wasn't enough for them

They mutilated kids and attacked those who disagreed
But it wasn't enough

They had laws protecting everyone except the white straight male
But it wasn't enough for them

They control the media ad deliberately lied time and time again
But it wasn't enough

The cheated in every election since JFK at least
But it wasn't enough

They lied about alternative energy
As it killed birds and wasted unrecyclable parts
But it wasn't enough

They create wars for money
Not giving a care about the soldiers
But it wasn't enough

They said they wanted to put brain chips in us to control us
To enslave humanity forever
And people laughed and said it was a conspiracy theory
They openly said they wanted to genocide a race of people
But no one cared

Searching

My soul Is in hell without you
Heaven is hell without you
I have searched everywhere
For that one soul to complete mine
You're the only thing that matters

I looked and looked
Never knowing always believing
I tried and tired
Failing and failing time after time
But you gave me life

Never again will I suffer
For you will be mine forever
Never again will I long
Because you and I will be one
Forever

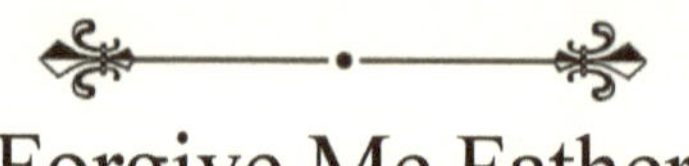

Forgive Me Father

I feel such pain
I feel such angst
I feel such hardship
But just the thought of you
Makes my day forever

I have no friends
I have no confiding
I have no god to protect me
But I have you
My beloved world

I need food
I need sleep
I need work
But more than that I need you

If we suffer together
We'll be stronger together
We'll bond tighter
We'll grow as one
We can handle the pain
So, we can handle the joys

If we're poor
We'll have more love
We'll share our worlds
We'll appreciate what we do have
We'll be riche together in our poverty
Eva I. LOVE YOU

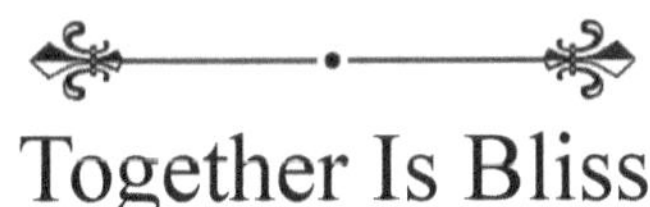

Together Is Bliss

I've cried
But the tears feel good
In retrospect it's heaven
Because they led me to you

I've died
In every way without you
You were meant for a better
But no one's as good for you as me

I can finally live
I can finally breath
Because I know your mine
Always and forever
We'll make earths hell paradise

Eves Rhyme

Eva you are the new eve
And I'm the new Adam
I'll take the fall
So, when we're banished
I'll comfort you

It's okay that you are curious
I'll take the blame
I'll take it upon myself
I'll be. the man
So, you can enjoy the forbidden fruit
We've become gods now

Power Hungry Woman

I never wanted godhood
But you did
It's okay I'll be your servant
The best gods are
Eva, I don't care what they promised
All I can offer is hardship
To suffer with me forever
But we'll make it!

We have each other
Eva my promises are the hard knock life
A life of pain and sorrow
I'm the god of sorrow the god of pain

But I'll keep it so you can be
The goddess of joy and pleasure
Eva I've died a thousand times
And been reborn a better man

You'll never have to feel hardship
I'll take it on myself
We're the yin and yang
Sorrow and joy

My Alpha Queen

Eva I've longed for you
But you need more than me
Theres only one me
I only have so much to offer

I'll give you the gift of motherhood
I need you to teach them
To guide and comfort them
I need you to lead

They need you more even I need them
I entrust you as the alpha queen
My quiet ace up my sleeve
Take care of my beloveds when I'm gone
I trust you
I love you
forever and always

Friends Come and Go...

I've tried
To be a friend
But friends come and go
The best the worst
They all come and go

I've been there
That friend that comes and goes
That wandering soul that says hello
As we touch tangentially
Forever connect forever gone

We come we go
Each passerby a possibility
Everyone's lonely but we got our backs
One day we'll have time
Time to say more than hello

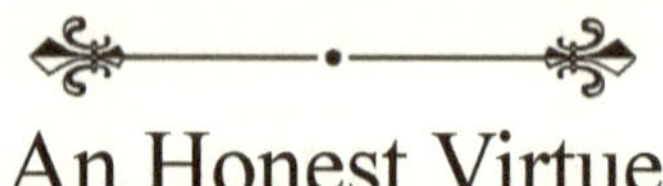

An Honest Virtue

Virtue is leaned under fire
As coal becomes diamond
So too does character
Ever changing at a moment's notice

Stay focused or we slip
Honesty is prime
Without it there can be nothing
We can't communicate

We can't function we can't live
Honesty keeps us from losing our inner truth
Why does one need virtue?
It's the key to life

Virtue is learned under fire
But useful always
Virtue sustains life
Being direct is a virtue

Ode to Politicians

What makes a good politician?
As we see them on television
A great actor is key
Saying: "believe me... you're free!"

Mayhap a cunning tongue?
Or getting nothing done?
Spending our fortune
while they fill their portion

Perhaps a mindless dummy
As it gets less sunny
And must sell its soul
To make its bank account full

They promise us, the herd,
That their opponents a turd
Having nothing positive
Serving only their prerogative

Goodbye lovely voters
They'll sell out their supporters
As they obey the rich
And dry their constituents like a lynch

The Least Shall Be the Greatest

L ittle soldier
Listen to the words commanded you!!
O ye of little faith
Will you hear this voice of comfort:
I Am …

Litter soldier
Listen to the words of mercy!!
Be strong and of good courage
Will you hear the words of comfort
This too shall pass

Little soldier...
Listen to the words of strength!!!!
I am with you always
Will you take the words of courage
Death where is they victory??

Heart of Stone

Emptiness of feeling
My heart is underwater
I sink like a stone
Engulfed by the water

Falling fast
Deeper and binding
Right is wrong
Amid constant winding

Ashamed of self
Nay – too deep
Let down by feeling
Unable to weep

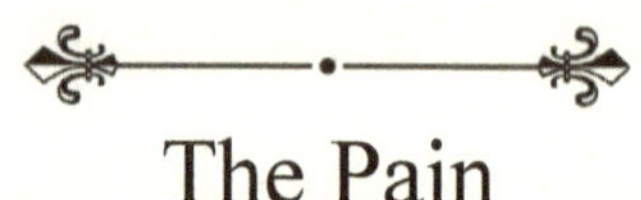

The Pain

I've cried a thousand tears
Wallowing in the pain of life
Seeking for a way out
A way to escape it all

And you dear child
You dear lover
You have nowhere to turn
No friend to comfort you

If I could take your pain I would
If I could do anything to help
You're the main reason for me
The yin to my yang
The life to my death
The love to my hate

Eva, I want your input in everything
I trust in you in absolute
I just wanna see you
I miss you so much
I LOVE you always and forever

Forgive Me….

Dear soul mate
Will you love me
When I go crazy
When I hear voices
When they tell me you're against me
Will you still trust me?

Dear soul mate
Will you love me
When I get depressed
When I feel empty
And don't wanna do anything
Will you still want me?

Dear soul mate
Will you be with me
Through thick and thin
So, when I'm at my worst
And forget my love
Will you still love me?

Shared Pain Shared Love

I wanted her
The epitome of perfection
Everything I wanted
And more still
But I thought she was
An angel a dream
A higher law

But she was better than dreams
She had suffered like me
She cried like me
She doubted like me
But now she believed like me
So, she gets me

Because she knows
What I've been thru
So, she can feel my hurt
We've been thru hell
To help each other thru the fires

Your Weakness Meets My Strength

I'm glad you get sad with depression…cause I can make you happy
I'm glad you cry…. so, I can dry your tears
I'm glad you get lonely… so I can be there for you
I'm glad you struggle… so I can fight by your side
I'm glad your weak at times… so I can carry you
I'm glad you feel sorrow… so I can comfort you
I'm glad you've had bad thoughts … so I can fill your mind with pleasant ones
I'm glad you love me… so I can love you back

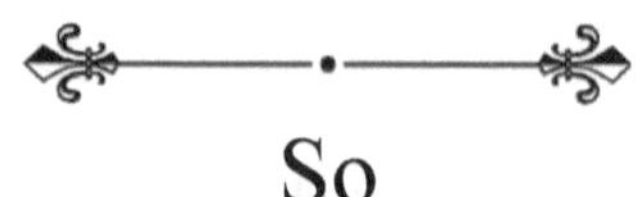

So

So
I wanted the world
Because she is the world
Everything else is just there
To entertain to serve to convenience us

So
I desired one earthly friend
But only that one
Because with a friend like her
Nobody else matters

So
I crave a relationship
That went above and beyond
That gave meaning purpose and depth
And she was then only one
The only one that understood me

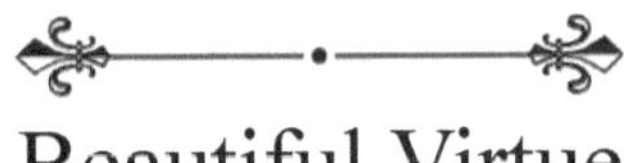

Beautiful Virtue

Rose fire
Your innocence
Your purity
Your sweet aura of presence
Lost but not forgotten
How you care!
You would heal the worlds sick
If you could
You would save the worlds lost
If they'd let you
You

Passion and understanding
A lover's lover
Who comprehends me
With a brilliant mine
I'm forever yours

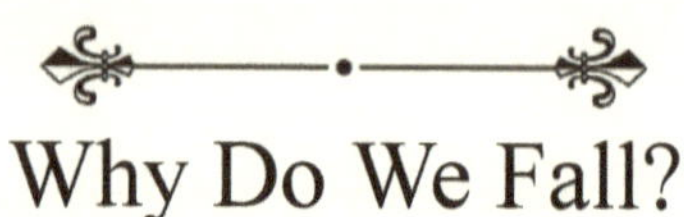

Why Do We Fall?

We all fall
But do we all get up?
It's the fall the deepens you
Until you hit rock bottom
Then you ascend beyond

We all lose
But do we all learn?
The failure teaches lessons
But do we gain understanding
Cause that's the purpose of losing

We all get nerves at times
Timid to the bone
We ain't always the brave and bold
But we level up each attempt
Until that which was frightening becomes commonplace

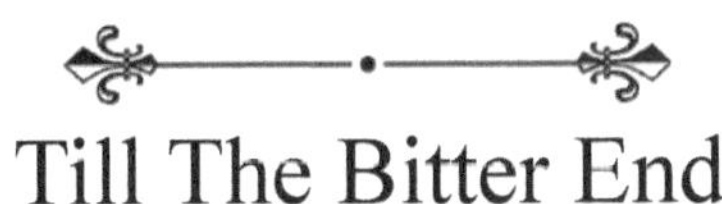

Till The Bitter End

My friend
I was there for you
You just didn't know
I wept for you

My friend
I never left you
Even in the worst time
I was by your side

My friend
I will never abandon you
I hate betrayal
I'll be your shadow

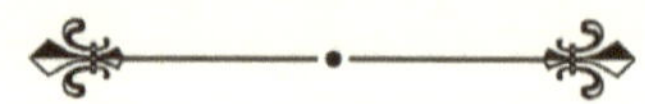

You Really Are My Equilibrium

I loved
You suffered
For me
I cried and it helped
You loved
I suffered
For you
You cried and it helped
We both took it upon our selves
To take the others pain
To carry a mile of the others struggles
So, we both understand
We both feel together
We both are one

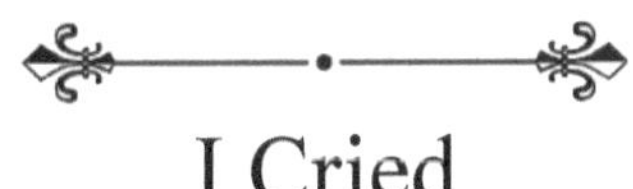

I Cried

I cried
My soul could finally express itself
The deep feeling of angst was exfoliated
The tears allowed the pain to leave the body

I laughed
My spirit was at ease for once
The deep weight of the world was reprieved
The spirit was able to express itself

I screamed
My heart finally let out all its anguish
The pain I felt was embodied in the noise
The heart was relieved of its crushing weight

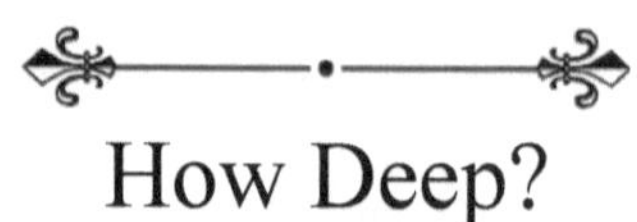

How Deep?

I once said I love you
But are you deep enough to know my love?
What good is depth if it can't be shared?
What good is a feeling if it can't be felt by another?
I will give you my love and make you comprehend my depth

I once said I cared
But do you understand the lengths id go for you?
what good is caring is the one doesn't receive it?
What good are the lengths if you don't come with me?
I will make your heart care for my length I go to woo you…

I once said forever
I meant that if time never ends… neither will my love for you
My love will grow stronger as I know you.
Our hearts will draw closer to one another
Our love will create peace amongst the nation a bliss amongst the people
But most of all… it will bind you and I as one … eternally

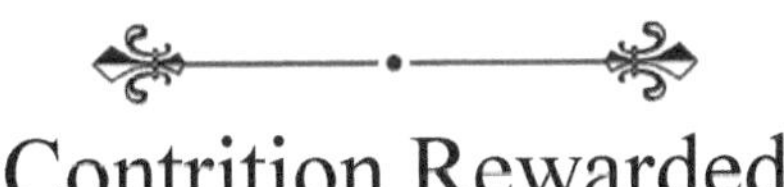

Contrition Rewarded

I knew it was wrong
The left field thoughts I had
Where I was of chief important
Or greater than the greatest
I could tell because
Only one Being sat above
And I'm not the Creator

I knew I was crazy
When the thoughts kept contradicting
When the voices repeated faulty logic
But how does one escape
When you're not in control
Thats where a Higher Power
Reminds you, "hey, I'm here"

I knew I had sinned
This way that way
And every-way in between
But you know what God showed me?
He said He looks at the heart
He studies the mind for deviance
And judges with utmost mercy
If they would just receive it

Tears of a Bystander

I wept
Over the pains of this life
Why does God
Make Children suffer?
I knew it was to humble the proud
To bring the haughty to kindness
To allow the hardest soul to mellow
But it still stung
I pray those kids be treated as martyrs

I balled
Why do the evil people run things?
Why are they in charge?
We must be evil as a race
Because anyone that gets to power
Sells out those they represent
Power without adhering to responsibility
Leads to suffering for all
They must be foolish cause they will be held accountable

I cried
Is there no woman for me?
No righteous companion
No better half gem
I gave up over and over again
I didn't want a normal wife
I wanted her… the one would complete me
If I never got her… I never would truly live
And the pain would never recede

Torment

I was trapped…
There was no way out
Trapped in my own devices
My own corruption
How can one conquer himself?
How can one overcome his humanity?
To be the hero one must crucify his own villain

I was lost…
There was no way to find a way out
No direction to lead
No guide to compass
How could I find my way out?
How could I decipher the invisible roadmaps?
To find your way forward you must know truth from fantasy

I was crushed…
Bones felt shattered
Muscles torn to pieces
Everything about me felt like I was dust and ashes
What could I do?
So, overwhelmed by life blows?

I'll Show You a Better Way

To take a stand you must conquer tiny problems until you can lift the big
Humanity is a dual edged sword
It was the humanity that taught me sin
This is the way
It'll be fun
What's wrong if no harms comes
Deceitfulness, pleasure and conceited mindset
All leading down a path of ruin
But

Humanity taught me repentance
You don't have to be evil
You can be forgiven
The contrition will help you amend
Transformation, humility, and a new set of eyes
All bringing hope to this troubled soul
Yet

My humanity brought redemption
I didn't have to stay in sin
I didn't have to be the villain
A sacrifice of one man
Brought forth the purity of billions
Glorious, power over self, and a loyal heart
Now and forever, we will reign as kings

Endure

Don't you dare give up
When you're on the edge
Barely able to move forward
When you have no way out
Don't you dare give up

Don't you dare give up
You'll never know
What if you hold on for just one more day
Miracles only happen to those alive
When you at a new low
Nothing seems right
And no man can uplift you
When all you have is pain and sorrow
Don't you dare give up

Don't you dare give up
If you do, you'll never remember
The joys that come after the lows
When you are discombobulated
Not knowing right from wrong
Not discerning forward from backward
Don't you dare give up now
People will help you along the way
Reality can come back to you
Miracles do happen
Don't you dare give up!

To Her

I just want to remind you
That even if you're not first
You are 1AAA
Next in line for my love and affection
Only God Is higher
I may have times of inward reflection
Where it seems like your invisible
But you're not; I see you
In the back of mind, you stick
I remember you and can't forget
I want you to know you're precious to me
that even on your bad days I see your beauty
in any frustration or indignation
I hold no grudges or ill-will
I only desire what's best for you
hopefully that's me
I love you still

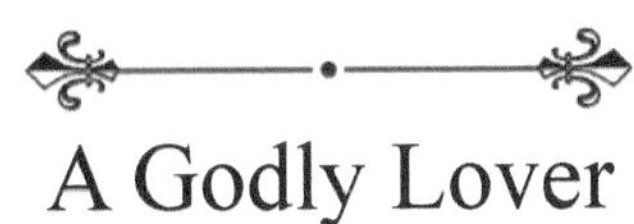

A Godly Lover

What do I like most about you?
I love your heart for God
Your heart desires to please Him
To follow His way with absolute zeal
Your love for His ways
And your commitment to Him

I love your genuine faith
True and authentic
Beautiful and full of solace
Steady and full of honesty
Through adversity strengthened and honed
Not trusting on yourself but Him

I love your passion
Your desire to be the great- and humble
Your desire to know Him in a deep personal way
Your dedication to follow Him as truly as possible
Your love of Him and others
And your willingness to suffer no matter what
Because you will never recant

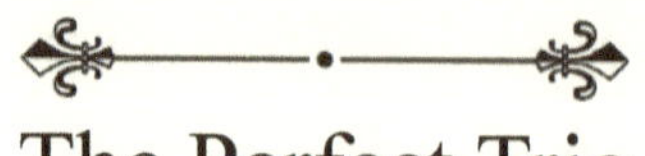

The Perfect Trio

I love you soul mate
Forever and ever
In this life and the next
Thru hell or in heaven
With pain or peace
Thru rain or sunshine
Lost or found
In too deep or on top
In over or heads or the perfect plan
Questioning life or solving puzzles
Away from you or with you
Thru space or thru time
In warmth or ice cold
When your alone I'll send my Savior
To comfort you with these words
I, Sergio Felix Nicene, LOVE YOU
And that's as constant as mankind will ever get
And ME YOU AND JESUS WILL BE TOGETHER FOREVER
Because the only being that loves you more
Is God

For You, I'd Lay Down My Life…I Only Ask you Follow in My Footsteps

I'll play the fool
To make others wiser
I'll be weak
to all others to rise up

I'll run
so, others can learn to fight

I'll follow
so, leaders can come forth

I'll guide
so, you can excel

I'll teach
so, you can thrive

I'll humble myself
so, you can be exalted

I'll serve you
so, you stand up with power

I'll minister
to train you in the way

I'll transcend friend
to become brother

I'll sacrifice my goals
so, you can reach yours

I'll lay my life down for you
that you may follow in my footsteps

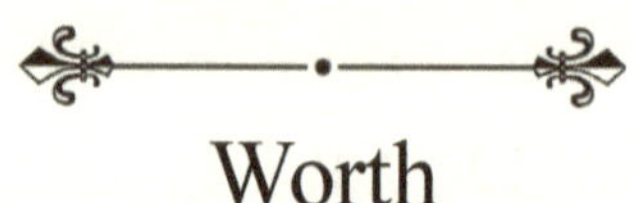

Worth

If you someone told you "You don't matter"
They have no idea what they're talking about
There is a God and He gives life meaning
As a King gives his constituents meaning
As a father his sons and daughters
As a Boss his employees
All life has meaning in this

God is the Father of mankind
And we have the ability to be His children
To be as He is without blemish
To be as He is humble and great all at once
To be men and women of character and inward beauty
To be children of the light
Glorious spirits that shine as the sun

So, the next time someone says you don't matter
You tell them if you don't matter neither do they
But even the vilest sinner can change from no purpose
To a life of dedication and depth
So that even if the devil himself would repent
God would forgive
And bring meaning back to his life

Woman Make Me Your Second Love

Woman do you love me?
listen to the words of Jesus

Woman, do you care about me?
Then follow the Bible

Woman, will you serve me?
Then serve the living Savior

Woman, will you do my will?
Then follow the will of the Father

Woman, will you stand by me?
Then stand by the Christ

Woman, will you leave all for me?
Then leave all for Christ

Woman, will you follow my teachings?
Learn the ways of the Word of God

Woman will you be my partner in this life?
Seek out the Creator

Woman, will you walk and talk with me?
Do so with the Prince of Peace

Woman will you be faithful until death to me?
Live for the Savior of mankind

Woman will you be mine forever?
ALWAYS REMEMBER TO PUT GOD FIRST
Amen

Simple Folk Great Rewards

I waved greatness by
Greatness passed me by
I waved
It mocked me for being nothing
For lowering myself
But I laughed at it with my friends
Knowing it would never understand
The value of lowliness

Genius passed me by
I waved
It laughed at me for being so simple
I just enjoyed the sunshine
And the company of similar minded folk
Who cares about genius
Especially if you're not happy

Power passed me by
I waved
It said I had no way to change the course
I enjoyed the limited responsibility
I said I just trusted God'll work it out
And pitted him for his blindness
Because power comes from the masses

I learned to Praise Him

Pain came upon me
I begged death to take me
I pleaded and pleaded
but death said
"God won't let me take you "
So, I cursed God

Sorrow came upon me
I begged death to take me
I pleaded and pleaded
But death said
"God won't let me take you"
So, I cursed God

Loneliness came upon me
I begged death to take me
I pleaded and pleaded
But death said
"God won't let me take you"
So, I cursed God

I felt immense satisfaction finally
No more pain sorrow or loneliness
I was happy I had everything I could dream of
Death came to take me
I said "but I have so much to live for
Please please let me stay!!"
"I'm not the one calling you home," said death
and I praised God for the last time

Without Understanding Way?

I got in an argument
My words are Greek to them
Their words were Latin to me
While the audience spoke Mandarin
What's the point of arguing without comprehension?
Yet thus is most arguments:
You don't try to understand you try to prove

I got in a feud
We saw things as different
As roman gods vs Norse mythology
We fought like bitter rivals
But what's the point of a feud without compromises
Unless one is completely off their rocker
Or ones in absolute truth
Usually there's gotta be give and take

I found a solution
But no one understood
It was as foreign to them as Antarctica
I tried explaining
But none could see
What's the point of understanding
When no one else does?
Who does that help?

Nothing Lasts Forever

I played the fool
Everyone saw me
They laughed and pointed
Everyone said they'd never forget
Until they did
People couldn't even remember my name

I saved the day
Everyone knew
They praised and hollered
They said I was the best
Until they forgot
And no one praised me anymore
There were new heroes

We were great friends
Inseparable
Always together never apart
We would be friends forever
Until time kicked in and I moved
I raised a family and he was just a thought
In the back of my ever-changing mind

Emotions Are Hard to Express

Tell me what you're thinking
They asked bug eyed
It's hard to convey emotions to thought
Cause my thoughts are frantic
They follow my ineffable emotions
Let's just say I'm conflicted

Tell me how you feel
They asked bug eyed
If I could tell you how I feel
I'd be a genius
It's like a game or riddle if you will
Deciphering my own emotions

Tell my why?
They asked bug eyed
Why is it hard to tune into your emotions?
I told them trying to explain yourself
Is one the most complex thing out there
I don't understand why I am what I am
If I did, I wouldn't be talking to you

Repetition Shows What's Important to You

I told them I loved them
They said okay
I told them no you don't get it
I LOVE YOUS
They said they got it
I said no yours missing the point
I GREATLY LOVE YOUS
They said they got it the first time

I said no you don't understand
The level of love I have for you
They said they kinda did
I said prove it
They said you love us
But how much I asked?
More than words can express or action can prove

I said but how deep?
They said higher than the heavens and deeper than the ocean
I wasn't satisfied
They didn't show me they understood
Until they said in sincerity and heart
I LOVE YOU TOO

You Still Don't Understand How Much I Love You Woman…

I loved her madly
But I wanted to emphasize
I wanted to make a point
On how much I loved her
She said she knew that
I didn't think she got it

I showed her everyone in the world
I said I love you more than these
I showed her how much I loved each one
And said I love you more
She said she already knew
I didn't think she got it
I tried to prove my love
In this way and that

It was never enough for me
Like an addict to his drug
I seek to love her more
Drilling it into her conscious and soul
Until she finally gets it
What does it take to prove my love?
I separate myself from women
Stop looking at them entirely (as best I can)
I want you and your alone

Do you comprehend my love?
Does my language speak to you?
What does it take to prove my love?
I write letters to explain. it
I craft poems to convey it

All this is for you
Do you comprehend my love?
Does my language speak?

What does it take to prove my love?
If I were emperor id put you over my kingdom
If I was a trillionaire id put you in charge of my money
Everything for you because I trust you
Do you comprehend my love?
Does my language speak?

Why Is Jesus So Quiet?

Jesus asked me where I was headed
I said I'm not sure
here's what I want though
He listened quietly

Jesus asked me why I wanted that
I said it makes me happy
It gives me satisfaction
He listened quietly

I talked for a bit
And He just listened
I asked why He didn't talk much
He said He was more interested in me than Himself

I asked Jesus why He didn't go after everything He wanted
He said He did
To prove His love eternally
He wanted to suffer for His creation
So, they knew how much they mattered to Him

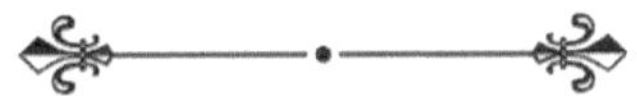

Let Him Who is Guilty Cast the First Stone

Death to the liar!!!
The hypocrites chanted!!!
Take away his seat
Burn his house down
His words were twisted
Hypocrites focus on honest men

Death to the blasphemer!!!
The religious men chanted!!!
Take away his seat
Burn down his house
He doesn't deserve life
As they missed the whole point

Death to the guilty man!!!
The flawless ones ordered!!
Take away his seat
Burn his house down
Because only the guilty
Bear the weight of their sins

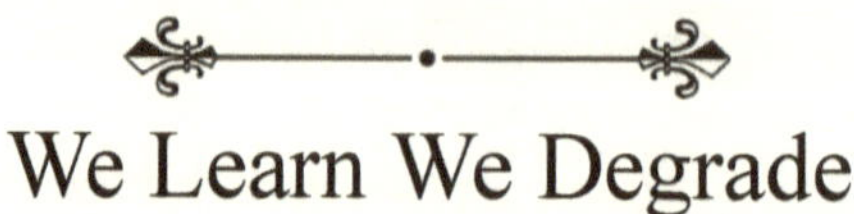

We Learn We Degrade

I was taught to speak
So, what did I learn to do best?
Swear like a sailor

I was taught to walk
Where did I run to most?
To get into fights around town

I learned to drink water
Yet what did I learn to drink in age?
Hard liquor from the bar

I learned to love
What did I love above all else?
Me myself and I

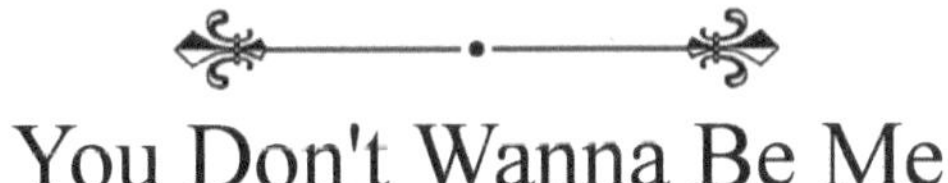

You Don't Wanna Be Me

They loved me
My family friends and acquaintances
But I hated what I was
They didn't know the demons I hid
They didn't know the monster inside
They didn't wrestle with themselves like I did

They applaud me
Every win every prize every accomplishment
But I despised myself
I know I could do better
I know I was being held back
They saw greatness but I knew I could outdo it

They said I was everything they wanted to be
But I didn't want anyone to be like me
I didn't want them to have to suffer
To have to go the brink time and time again
To feel the desire to die repeat itself
I wanted good things for them- not my life

Notice

I saw her
She saw me
She turned around and left
I kept thinking about her
I spoke a word to her
She in turn spoke one word
Goodbye

I kept think about her
I asked why not me
She said we were oil and water
She didn't understand me
Otherwise, she'd keep thinking about me

Everyone needs compassion
I was alone
No friend
No brother
No ally
So, I stayed in my room
Until I was forced to make interaction

I was in isolation by default
I didn't want a friend
I didn't want a brother
I didn't want an ally
I was happy alone
Until I was made to understand

I came to an epiphany
Maybe they're just like me
No friend
No brother

No ally
And like me deep down
They just wanted someone that cared

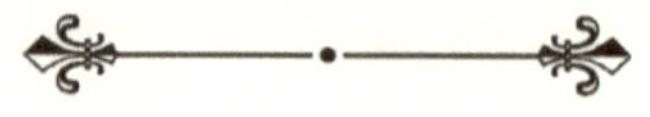

The Power of Forgiveness

I erred
I apologized
They forgave

I fought harder
I failed
I humbled myself
They forgave

I rose to new heights
I faltered
I lowered myself in shame
They forgave

I soldiered on
I sinned miserably
My heart fell into deep contrition
They forgave
I became a holy saint
Is this true?

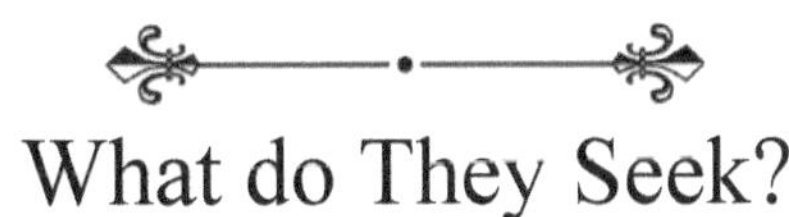

What do They Seek?

I had no idea what she wanted
I thought if I was smart, she'd want me
But she wanted relatability
No some puffy intellectual

I had no idea what she wanted
I thought if I was strong physically, she'd want me
But she said she wanted someone that could carry her emotionally
Not some useless strength that can't help her

I had no idea what she wanted
I thought she wanted the perfect saint; flawless
But she wanted someone like her that understood her faults
Not some high in the sky perfection who couldn't sin or understand

I had no idea what she wanted
I thought she wanted an alpha male
But she wanted a partner: someone equal not above
Someone who looks her in the eyes as equals not beneath them

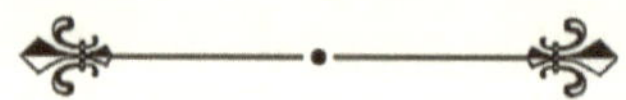

Every Failure is a Hidden Victory

I ran
But my feet stumbled
So, I crawled to the finish line
But I made it

I spoke
But my words were muffled
So, I lost my debate
But I went the distance

I tried
But my heart fell
I had lost all hope
But I heard a whisper
Every failure is a hidden victory

Adams Lamentation

Why do I exist?
Without her…why??
I only sow sorrow and reap defeat
Cause she completes me
And with her I rise to new heights

Do I exist for her??
Why was I created?
Lost and alone without her
Seeking satisfaction
That only she can fulfill
Pain torment, or …her?
Was I created for her sake?
How do I solve my equation?

The answer to if I'm alone in the universe
Without that perfect partner
I wander endlessly
I wonder fruitlessly
Seeking her, pondering if she's out there
What woman equals me; together perfectly balanced?

I have evidence; a proof
She exists because I do
She was created for me as I was for her
And I can't be alone in the universe
Because I have burning passion
That only she can fulfill
She is the lifeblood to my soul
The beauty that awakens my sight
And the passion that satisfies my thirst
Sorry for my idol God…maybe one day it will go away … forgive me

Heavy Lies the Crown

Who desires the seat of the Most High?
To be responsible for all creation
To have to weigh men in the balance
To decide right from wrong
To command angels' men and creatures
Trillions upon trillions of thoughts to hear
The entire universe held up by your power
Why would anyone wanna be God?
Who wishes they were the Creator?
With none to council you as you create
As big as Jupiter as minuscule as an atom
Language and math; music and writing
The human body so delicately interwoven
With mind body soul all into one finite being
So, complex we will never fully understand it
Why would anyone wanna be God?

Who wants to create the laws of mankind?
Find the perfect law that applies to all creation
Laws of science math and music
Laws of nature that cannot be defiled
So complex and distinguished
Even the most skilled minds will never fully comprehend
And above all the moral law of mankind
Who has the wisdom to create the perfect way to life?
Why would anyone wanna be God?

The Devil and God Are Raging Inside Me

How can a cell be greater than the man???
And how can a man be greater than God?
If the Bible is riddled with half-truth…
|Where does one begin and where does one end??
Is there any truth to it if there's a possibility of lie?
What precisely is the half-truths and how are they?
I'd almost takes more comfort if God judged me horrifically in this life…
Than to go to the next life and find out God isn't all He's cracked up to be….
Have mercy on me great Creator!!!

Can Vices Destroy Honest Men?

Liars lie
But so do honest men
No one could completely tell the truth
At least honest men try
And are willing to admit they were wrong
Can anyone always speak truth? I used to think God and God alone

Everyone's selfish
To a degree
You need your needs first
You care about your life greater than a stranger
If we didn't society would collapse
Just take care of the youth first or there's not a future

Hatred enters the heart
Of someone or of something
Despises them for their deeds
Bad men hate good deeders
Good man hates the evils works
And sometimes even hatred creeps in
And consumes a good man
Making him evil

This is All My Mind Going Crazy Forgive Me World

I sought for love
The romantic type but so much more
Sparks flying inside us forever
Feelings on overload perpetually
Talking and writing our language being the core
And being together the centerpiece

Of course, I'd like to touch
To feel her everything
But I want so much more
Her company her personality
Her brilliance her creativity
I want her whole being and to give her mine

Just a man and a woman
Who loved each other more than others
Who complimented each other to a T
Who had depth each individually
So that when they collided, they went as deep
As a black hole, with no ending

Right and Wrong are Diagonally and Orthogonally

Good and evil and both half truths
And gravity run amok
What is the meaning of this all?
Who can tell the right direction?
When maps are written in Latin
And roads in spheres
How can I know where to go?
Who can know the correct love?
When I dunno how love looks…
And I've never met her or seen her…
Will my heart betray me?

The Greater love

There was love
Love for country
Love for freedom
Love for the stars and stripes
But love for her was greater

There was love
Love for family
Love for brethren
Love for blood and race
But love for her was greater

There was love
Love of life
Love of victory
Love of the unknown
But love for her was greater

There was a love
Of people
Of ideologies
Of possibility
But none of that mattered
Without her by my side

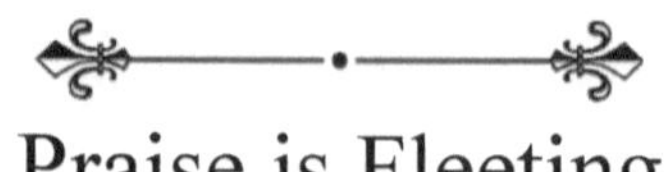

Praise is Fleeting

If I could have the greatest minds
Praise and elevate me
For my talents skills and ideas
I'd give a hard pass
I'd rather be the great mind elevating others

If I could have a partner
Woo me and adore me
And talk about why they love me
I'd tell her sorry babe
It's my job to elevate you
And let you know just how much you mean to me
(But if it comes from the heart …
She better expect a greater love from me
Because she is why I am that great)

The one praise that matters is if God Himself wanted to praise me…
I'd accept it as nothing is greater than the praise of God
For it is perfect and without blemish or bias
Yet He alone deserves all adoration glory and praise
I'll praise You for your handiwork and grand plan
Yet more than praise I just need to know you love me and that is sufficient
Because your worth isn't based on how much you're praised
But how much your most dear ones love you
And love is weightier than praise

Iron Sharpens Iron

She makes me pure cause she's pure
She makes me wise to guide her
She makes me a lover to woo her
She makes me strong and brave to protect
For what is action without an equal reason to act for?

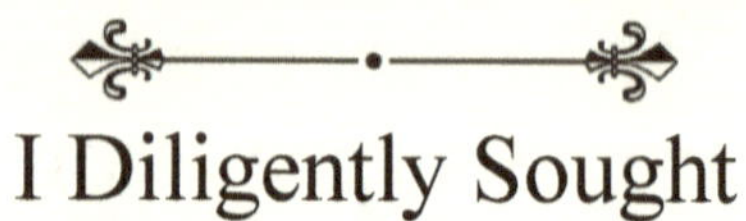

I Diligently Sought

I searched for answers using facts
They said everything anyone wanted
But when I got down to it
It wasn't about fact or evidence
But what one believed

I sought questions to uncover truth
Every question had already been asked
But not all were answered
Yet I learned the best answers
Just lead to more questions

I desired understand using wisdom
Seeking the Words of God
Wisdom, it turns out
Isn't an action or feeling
But a way of life

Where the Hats of Humans Head

Human beings
All go their own way
One to work
Another to play
All ask for directions
As we see dozens come and go
What binds us is our connections

Family members
Most desire peace like a dove
As they go about their lives
Fighting each other in what should be love
The binding together force
Compassion mercy understanding
May repair the wounds at the source

Lovers
Man and beautiful wife
Bound together as one
Living thru the struggles of life
Seeking the best for one another
Growing together daily with purpose
They discover depths of each other

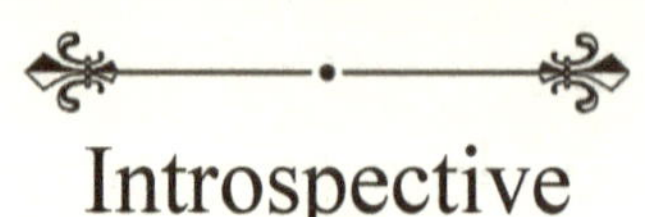

Introspective

I never knew who I was
I sought from books media and art
It showed me what I could be
But not what I am

I sought to know myself
So, I sought friends and family
They showed me I belonged
but couldn't take me where I desired

I sought religion
It said the Greatest gave a care
It got me thru some
But there was a still a hole

I had a burning hole within
A desire for an equal counterpart
Something that truly fulfilled
Ss Adam was empty without Eve
So too do I need her
Forgive me God for my idolatry

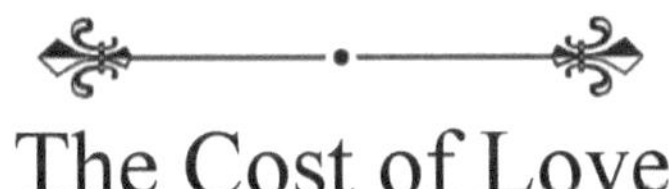

The Cost of Love

Love Is demanding
It demands our focus
It demands our attention
It demands details
So why do we crave it?

Love is costly
It costs time
It costs effort
It costs opportunities
So, we do we desire it?

Love is painful
We see them suffer helplessly
We leave them for time without choice
When we screw up it hurts us like it hurts them
So why do we need it?

We crave it
Cause it completes us
We desire it
Cause it fulfills us
We need it because
The highs outnumber the lows

The Leader Paradox

I think I'd be a horrible leader
Because I hate violence
I don't wanna have to end another life
Or hold the power between life or death
I don't wanna control people
And tell them what to do
Unless its morality or sound law
I want them to freely choose
And I certainly don't wanna spy
Know everything my people are doing
It's their life and I need evidence
I'd rather not know if it doesn't hurt people

I do wanna woo women to be mothers
I do wanna let men excel and provide
I do want kids to be protected
And taught morality of the Bible
I do want criminals put away
So, they can't harm people
I do want our culture to be pure
For marriages to stick for things to be kid friendly
I do want hard workers
And dedicated loving parents
I do want normalcy; no more pagan
No more tats and nose rings or fornicators

Who Determines Worth?

ill I ever be enough
I have high aspirations
Not precise not detailed
But greatness in my eyes
Will I ever achieve it?

I hope to transform the world
To change all for the better
To live a life that relates
And takes people to new heights
But when will I attain?

When will I get the point
That I tell myself well done
Will it ever be enough?
Does my opinion matter?
And Who determines worth?

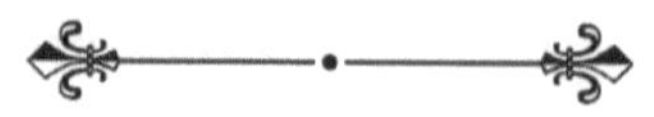

Dreams of a Lover

My dream
My fantasy dream
Her
To be a reliable man
For her
To be wealthy
So, she's not poor
To be strong
So, she can lean on me
To be wise
So, we can communicate
To be funny
So, she can laugh
To be clever
So, her brains engaged
To be patient
So, she can grow
To be subtle
So, she can shine
To be holy
So, she doesn't leave me behind
To be humble
So, she can relate
To be brave
So, she's protected
To be honest
So, she can trust me
To be worthy of her
So, there's equilibrium
To be other for her always
So, she understands how much she means to me
To listen to her
So, I can know her better

To give her her dreams
So, mine can come true

Good Times Bad Times Thru and Thru

I wanna make her laugh
And be there when she cries
Cause every emotion to me
Is a thing of beauty

I wanna see her in joy
And comfort her in sorrow
Cause she's got so much too her
I wanna see every amazing side

I wanna experience her goofy side
And be there when she doesn't make sense
Cause those make the best stories
And time and time again bring smiles

I wanna see her at her best
And be there when she's feeling the worst
Cause she needs a strong man
To understand so he can be there for her
I wanna show her the world
And watch her marvel
Cause she's my world
And never disappoints

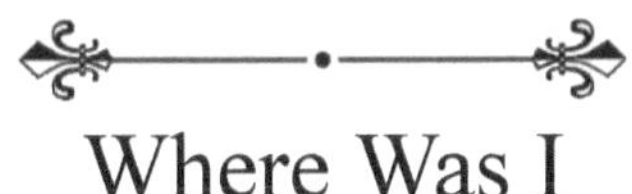

Where Was I

I'm sorry
I was never there for you
When you were fighting
Your hardest battles
I shoulda found a way
Please forgive me

I wrote to you here from my cushy seat
While you went crazy
And sought me like a detective
I shoulda done more to find you
I'm just a bum forgive me
I'm sorry I just kept writing
And writing and writing

While your heart was crushed
By my disappointing inaction
One day I'll make it all up to you

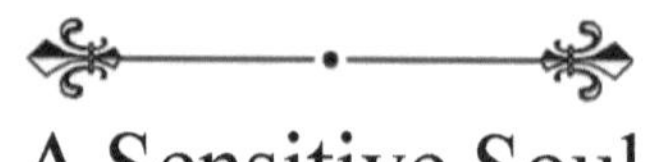

A Sensitive Soul

I know I may not have done anything wrong…
I just feel bad...
Like I truly did let you down…
Like I'm not doing enough…
Like I'm not carrying my half of the weight…
I'm a sensitive guy woman…
You gotta understand…
If you show any signs of upset or frustration …
I'll be worried all day I did something wrong…
Just let me know if I've wronged you and I'll try to make it right, okay???
The last thing I want is for anything to come between us…

Your Gravity vs the Worlds Weight

I could embarrass myself beyond measure
To the whole world
But if you reassured me
Like "they don't matter"
Or "I thought it was funny"
I'd believe you

I could say the lamest things
Look the fool in absolute
That they'll all forget
I wouldn't care
Cause they'd all forget

If I wrote my heart's content
For the world to see
Every speck of me
I'd want them. to think I was crazy
I'd want them to think I was mad
I'd want. them to think I was lovesick
For you and only you

What Do I Desire from You?

Well you already have
The perfect soul and
The perfect body
You're the perfect girl
In my eyes at the least
So, I just desire you be
Your perfect self

But I'll ask you give me
As much time as you
Can spare this poor soul
To give me wealth

Your time is worth more
To me than all the riches
Lastly, I ask you humor me
You let me take you on fancy dates
You let me buy you flowers gems and chocolates
You let me go places and do things with you
At least read my writings
And mayhap write me back so we can bond

You let me listen and share your hearts treasures with me
Let me be there for you
It's the man in me that wants to do all this
Let me be your man
Forever

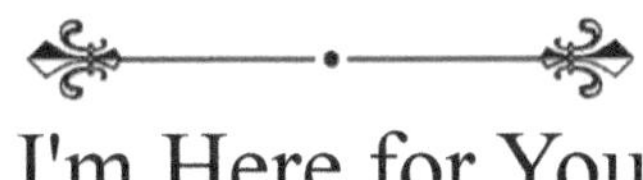

I'm Here for You

When sorrow enters your soul,
My soul will take your sorrow
And replace it will laughter
I'll be there for you
In sunshine or rain

When anxiety fills your emotions
my presence will calm you
And fill your emotions with peace
I'll be there for you
Through thick or thin

When insanity takes over your mind
I will give you logic
And bring your mind back to reasoning
I'll be there for you
Through sanity or a lost mind

When pain fills your body
My words of comfort and cheer
Will make your body forget the pain
I'll be there for you
In laughter or tears

When death stings your heart
My love of life will bring you back
Forgetting your loss and remembering hope
I'll be there for you
In life or death

Awaken Strengthened

One day I woke up
Depressed without end
It's a constant battle
But a constant victory
Because it always makes me stronger

One day I woke up
Voices in my head condemning me
I fought it won and got it again
It consumed me and taught me
No battle is ever truly over
So, it made me wiser and battle tested

One day I woke up lonely
Without a woman to call my own
A hole in my heart that only she could fill
I searched but couldn't find; waited but nothing
But when I find her, everything will add up
All my pains will mean little when I say
One day I woke up next to her happy

One day I woke up meaningless
Empty shallow and depraved
No depth no higher purpose
No way forward or direction
Until He found me
Spiritually naked and ashamed
He said "My Spirit can heal
My fellowship is comfort
And my grace is sufficient"
So I suffered with joy for the Lamb

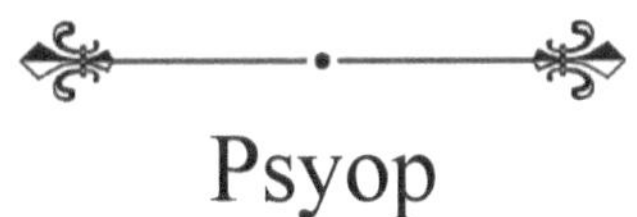

Psyop

It was a war of the mind
Psyop at its finest
No one even knows
Who's waging war with whom

You don't know who is good or bad
Because it's always the same people
With no dissenting opinion
Collusion at its finest

The good of twenty years ago
Is evil today- worse than their wrongs
While todays evil was never good before
We learned from our mistakes they say

Control to the point
You don't know how to break free
From inside the matrix
They are who they say they are

If he lies, they lied about his lies
If he stumbles it was his fault
No one is right or wrong we're all in the gray
Except you- your always wrong when you disagree

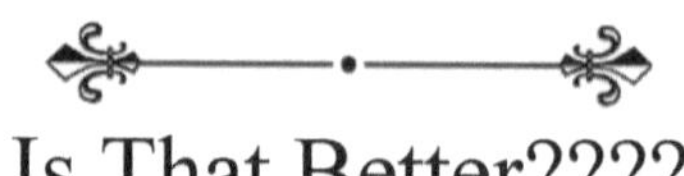

Is That Better????

Why do I love her- the unknown
Why do I love a woman I've never met
Because I believe she loves me dearly
I believe she'll take care of me
I believe she'll sacrifice for me
And I believe she fill this hole

I believe she is made for me
And I for her (I don't want her pulling all the weight)
Why do I love a woman I've Never seen?
Because I believe she's beautiful
In every deep way possible
Because I need her to bring
Light, beauty, and grace
To reach this hardened soul
And give me life again

Why do I love a woman I've never talked to
Because I know we'll connect
It'll come easy to converse
To reach her soul with words
Because she'll bring out the best in me
As one mind alone gets lonely
And she fills my emptiness with life

The Adulterous Doctor

They had a dream
It ended up a nightmare for me
They dreamed of equality
It only led to inequality for my people

They dreamed of multiculturalism
It led to a near genocide of my people
They dreamed of women's rights
It destroyed men and women

They dreamed of sexual rights
It led to pedophilia
They dreamed of power to help
It led to power to destroy

They dreamed of helping refugees
It made us minorities on our own land
They dreamed of healthcare
It led to corruption and death

They dreamed of reparations
It led to slavery
They dreamed of a world government
It led to less power and fewer right

They dreamed of a genocide of whites
Will whites fight back?
Or do they believe we are all God's children?

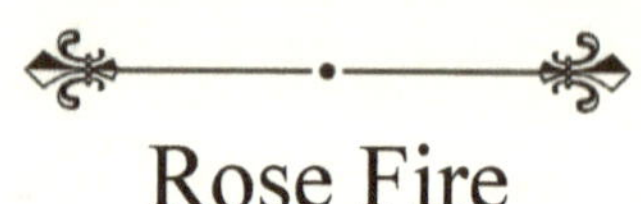

Rose Fire

R ose fire,
You burn my soul afire
The flames you create in me
Are the engine that moves me
Pushing me to go farther
And love deeper

Because of you
You soothe my soul like water
Easing my tensions
And creating peace within
Just knowing that you
Are mine and I am yours

Our harmony is smooth like water
You shine forth on my soul
Like the sun in the heavens
Helping me believe truth
And see the world anew
Reminding me that
Holiness is attainable

Sparks of Destiny

You
    It was always you
    From the get go
I uttered your name
As if you were all mine

How did I know
I thought you were too good for me
Only a higher being would be worthy of you
I still don't know why you'd choose me
But that's why I doubted

I didn't think I was good enough
But I all comes full circle
The only romance I had
Wasn't far away in another galaxy
But you
The one that I was made for
The one that completes me
The one that always knew

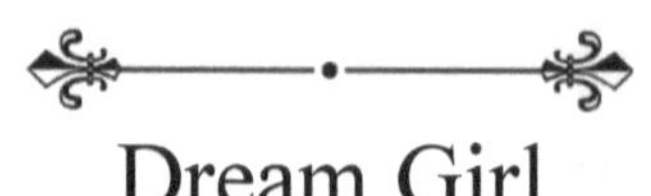

Dream Girl

Why?
why am I willing
To punish myself
Just to see you smile?

Time and time again
I'd go beyond pain
For your happiness

Why will I
Do the things I'd do
For no one else
Push myself
Just to satisfy her

To give her what she wants
Whatever that may be
Why does she
Make me feel alive?

Take me to another world
Where every smile
Makes the neurons fire
And every conversation
Brings out more dopamine
Than the highest high

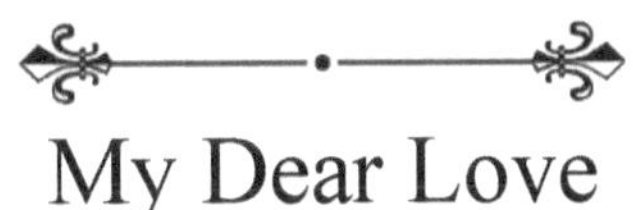

My Dear Love

Dear one
There's been
Troubled times
Troubled minds
Troubled hearts
But when we meet
All will be water under the bridge

Dear one
There's been
Confusion
Deception
And lies amok
But all will be revealed
And sanity restored at your appearance

Dearest one
There's been
Hopes
Dreams
Heartfelt desires
And the only answer to them
Is you
Searching for my dream soul

The Fiery Soul of Virtue

I searched valiantly
Upwards downwards
In every direction
Both ways reversed
But she wasn't there
My fiery soul of virtue

I left my home
Left everything
Just to know her name
But I couldn't find out
Anything about her
My righteous woman of piety
Was she real?
A figment of imagination?
Could someone I dreamt of
Become reality?

Can you change your insides
To be as beautiful as God?
Why did you choose me
I gazed at her perfections
And could only think of
My own imperfections
How I didn't deserve her
I wished she would find
Someone actually worthy

I noticed her perfect soul
Her uncanny kindness
Her eternal compassion
Her astonishing mercy
And I said I hope she finds

Someone she deserves

She said "I want you"
I looked around bewildered
"But I'm ugly inside" I said "and have issues"
She looked at me and said,
"I chose you because I love you
How could I be wrong?"

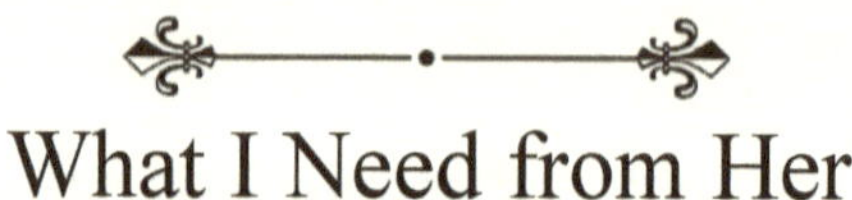

What I Need from Her

My better half I need
I need affection
From the one I love most
Because I need her assurance
That I matter

I need time
From my beloved
Because without her
Time is empty

I need forgiveness
From my dear lover
Because if she doesn't
I can't forgive myself
From wronging the purest soul
It's all for you my love

If my poems make you happy
I pray they never cease
Because they are written
For you
And your satisfaction

If my quotes intrigue you
I hope they go on forever
Because I want that mind
All on me
Cause my minds all on you

If my letters excite you
I'll never stop writing them
As a new day bring new possibilities

So, do you
Bring magic eternally

The Ultimate Creative

I wonder
Alone with no other consciousness
No beast no man no cell no spirit
What would I think?
And how? what would I think about?
My mind hurts thinking about it

I ponder
Outside of past present future
How could I create time?
And be inside it
And what would lead to me to make it?
My mind hurts thinking about it

I consider
Without space or matter
What would inspire that
How creative Is time
To make? what a foreign concept
My mind hurts thinking about it

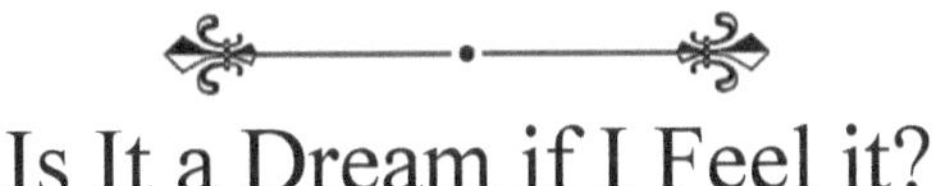

Is It a Dream if I Feel it?

I never met her
But I knew she was real
Because my heart is in pain
And there's always a solution
For love sickness

I didn't know about her
But I knew she was mine
Because I cared
So deeply about her
Someone must reciprocate

I didn't know why
Why she loved me
But I knew she did
Because my love
Needed a match

Love of Destiny

Twas foretold; in a way
Before I was born
Unbeknownst to all
The earth was preparing
For the love an age
You and me

Before you were born
I heard a whisper
Telling me
She'll be there
Wait and see

Before the earth
Before the stars
Before time
There was a thought called love
(You and me)
Destined to be together forever

Trillion to two
Trillions of souls
Living dead and immortal
All seeking a form of love
With only one soul
Belonging to me

Billions of lovers
Or at least together
Jealous of you and me
Cause they'll never have
The level of love we do

Millions of stories
Telling of love and romance
But all pale in comparison
To the beauty of our love

A Faithful Fabled Fantasy

You and me the probability
What are the chances
Of one man
And one woman
To be perfect for each other?
Cause we beat those chances;)

What are the odds
If a nobody guy
Making the most perfect girl
Fall for him?
Cause I beat those odds;)

What's the possibility
Of the whole existence
Life of all sorts
Elevating us beyond measure?
In my mind they have already;)

My Sweet Rose Fire…. The Beauty of a Rose and the Passion of a Fire

My sweet rose fire
The beauty of a rose
Personified in a woman
Unrivaled beauty among flowers
Unrivaled beauty among women
My sweet rose fire

My sweet rose fire
The passion of a fire
Unceasingly warm to your lover
Giving everything to me
Even when I don't deserve it
Always making up for my flaws
My sweet rose fire

Red Red Never Dead

Red red never dead
The color of love
Because not even I
Know the levels of love
Your depth reaches

Red red never dead
The color of passion
Because not even I
Understand the lengths you'd go
To save me

Red red never dead
The grave cannot hold you
Death is under your control now
Thank you
For choosing me
Thank you eternally

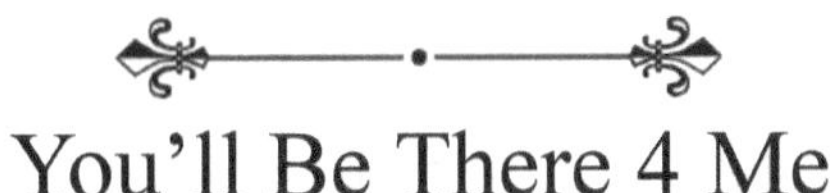

You'll Be There 4 Me

The thought of you
Keeps me going
Day by day I'm reminded
Just knowing you're out there
Fills me with hope

I don't wanna live
Not without you
But with you
Aye I could live forever

Without you by my side
This burning hole
In my heart
Aches and tears
My heart needs a home
And it only fits with yours

What Good Is Woman Without Man?

What good is the strength of men
If they don't protect women?
What good is masculinity
Without femininity to compliment

What good is logic and rationality of men
Without women's complexity

What good is men's hard work
Without providing for more than just himself

What good is man's romance
Without lovers to intake it

Want good is a man's legacy
Without his seed and the seed-bearer

What good is leadership
Without a woman to impress and obey

What good are men's eyes
Without a woman beauty to behold

What good is a loving heart
Without one to love and cherish

What good is a man's memory
Without anniversaries and birthdays of her

The Good Pharisees

The Bible says
The preacher said
Love your enemy
So, he killed me

The Bible says
The preacher said
Turn the other cheek
So, I lost my house

The Bible says
The preacher said
Obey the government
So, I lost all my rights
And lived in a totalitarian society

The bible says
The preacher says
There Is neither jew nor Greek
So, neither was there white anymore

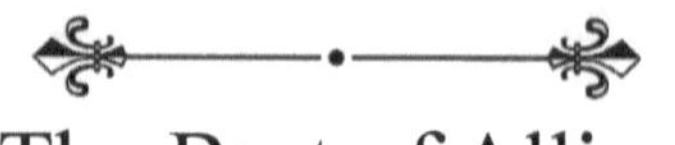

The Best of Allies

Why do the enemies
Want me to perish
But rather
Why do the friends
Wish me to fall?

Why do the friends
Abandon me
But rather
Why do some
Stand by during fire

Why do I seem so alone
With no one there
But rather
Why do so many
Seem to care
About a wandering soul like mine?

I thought they'd all hate me
Condemn me
Crucify me
Send to the prisons
But they didn't
Why?

I thought they'd see me as a threat
A man who speaks his mind
Not caring about
Being right in another
Just that he can speak his mind
No one came

They must at least agree
With some of my words
Or at least be willing to defend it
The ability to speak your mind
Whatever the case
Thanks for not hating me

I'd Still Love You

I still love you
Even if we go thru war
Blood everywhere
Violence amok
Terrible fates in the balance
I'd still love you

I'd still love you
Even if a better woman came by
Superior to you in beauty
I'd say she doesn't belong to me
Never knew her never wanted her
Besides my woman got a better soul
I'll still love you

I'd still love you
Even if I lost my mind again
I'd remember you as my only
I'd be in pain for everything but you
Harkening to you my love
I'd still love you

I'd still love you
If you got old and aged
Even if you looked worn
Without that outward beauty
I'd remember our time together in bliss
I'd still love you

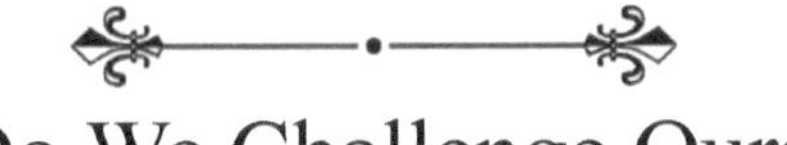

Why Do We Challenge Ourselves

They took the challenge
They climbed the mountain
Some mocked saying why?
But they'll never understand
The sense of accomplishment
The wonder of standing tall
Above all of creation looking down

They fought the battle
The war of the soul
They became better men
Better soldiers against their
Wicked instinct that pushes them
Towards beast and away from human

They won her over
Each to their own
The girl of their dreams
Waiting for them in virtue
Making their whole life change
With the joys and splendor
That only beautiful souls can reach together

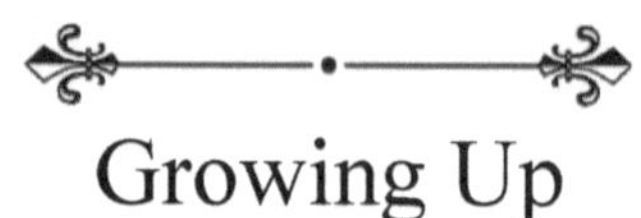

Growing Up

Why do we push ourselves
To new limits day by day
We grind not to thrive
We grind to survive
Getting by is a challenge

Why do sacrifice
Our dreams hope and desires
We were once young and hopeful
But life crushes you down
Leaving you with emptiness and pain

Why do we still hope
Still dreams of tomorrow
Things get better
We have to believe that
Without that spark of light
We are a pitiful forlorn race
We live we die, everyone
Our soul must be eternal
Or else where is the meaning?

Life of a Commoner

You're born
With love life enthusiasm
You love new things
You want to learn
Your to exited to dream of tomorrow
Because today is filled with so much

You grow
You gradually get bored
You rapidly lose interest
About as fast as you gained it
You dream of a better everything
Looking forward to tomorrow

You've grown
You don't have the energy you used to
You reminisce about the excitement of yesteryear
You dream of reliving your glory days
You wish you could do the things you used to
Alas it went by too quick; only memories remain
But what a gift life was!!!! Thank the Creator

To Those Who Seek Glory Worship and Praise

Those who seek glory
What good does that get you
In reality?
Some think your good at something
They praise you not for you
But for your accolades
If another raises above
You'll be forgotten

Those who seek worship
What good is it?
Are you our deity?
Is that what you want?
The same people that worship you today…
Will burn your house tomorrow
They don't care about your soul
They care about the latest greatest

Why do some people seek praise
Praise after all is fleeting
It comes and goes like the wind
And they will criticize just as fast
Why seek the praise of man
When you could have the camaraderie
Of another soul that actually cares from the heart

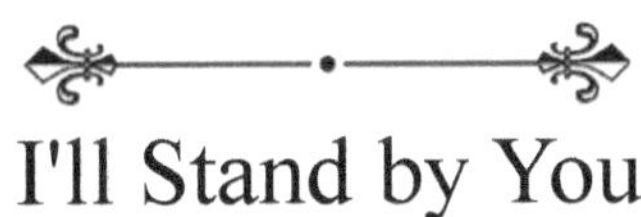

I'll Stand by You

I'll stand by you
   When the going gets tough
   I'll be there closer
Absorbing all the heat
To keep you safe
I'll stand by you

I'll stand by you
When all else forsake
Even if it's just us
I'll be there with you
To the very end
I'll stand by you

I'll stand by you
Through mocking and venom
Any malice towards you
I'll bear and replace
With love and laughter
I'll stand by you

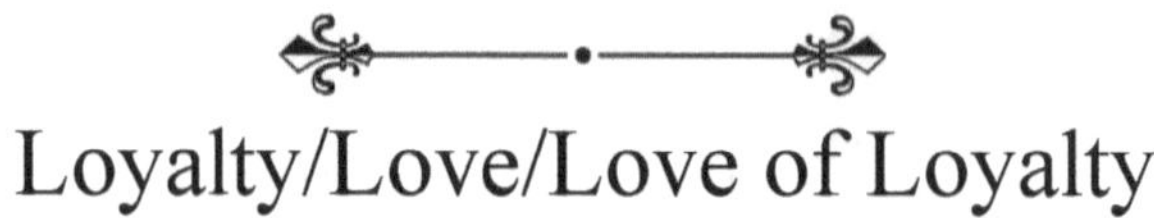

Loyalty/Love/Love of Loyalty

A friend will stand by you
A better friend will die before you
Leaving it all behind
As he smiles seeing you safe from harm

A lover has you
A better lover has no other
Eagerly awaiting you
As the joy of her life

A son listens to you
A better son obeys you
Trying to do the will of his father
Outta pure love for him

One Rose Has no Thorn

Every rose has a thorn
Is what they say
But they haven't met my love
She's complete rose without any thorn
Beauty without flaw
She's flawless

Nobody's ever seen the perfect diamond
It's beyond belief
Well, wait till you see my love
She has no imperfection
Shining forth as the sun
She impeccable

All humans are flawed
Everyone unique in their imperfection
But my love, my one-of-a-kind love
She's purer than the purest water
And doesn't know how to wrong
She's perfect

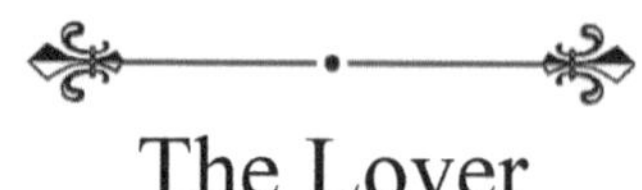

The Lover

I feel like I'm a born lover
Like I have so much love to give
But what good is all that bundled up
Without a women worthy of it?

I wanna pour it on your soul
I wanna love you with all I've got
My time and presence
My goofs and gaffes
My attention and dedication
I want you to experience the depth of love
I have for you and only you

I feel like I'm a natural giver
Giver of time words gifts
But without someone special
Someone I really wanna give too
Those gifts are futile

I wanna give you my everything
My heart and its tenderness
My mind and its depth
My soul and its love
I want you to have all of me
I wanna be with you forever
When I say forever, I mean It
When your old
If you ever lose it
I always want you by my side

I want to be hundred percent loyal
Through any trouble pain or trial
To see you through the dark times
To be by your side after millennia
Loving you in perfect harmony

Yesterday Was History Todays the New History

It's a new year
A time to be renewed
You are not the same person
You were last year
Shine brighter stand taller play harder

It's a new year
it's a chance to
Metamorphosis
Into something more
Deeper wiser and equipped for war

It's a new year
Let yesterday stay yesterday
Go farther reach higher dig deeper
Until you become
The dream you hoped for

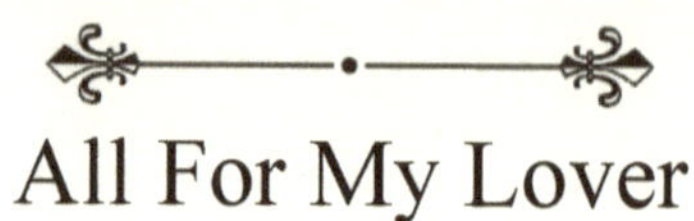

All For My Lover

If I could express my love with poetry
I would never run out of poems
My material would be a bountiful
As your beautiful soul
And your breathtaking body
Inventing new ways to say "I love you"

If I could express my love with gifts
I would buy you the priceless jewels
Bake and cook your favorite foods
Learn craftsmanship just to amaze you
But most of all
I'd give you all the time I could muster

If I could express my love with sacrifice
I'd give up my favorite hobbies just to spend time
I'd work multiple Jobs to provide
I'd kill all relationships with women
Yet nothing would be a sacrifice
Because I'd rather be with you
No matter the cost your worth it
What are you getting with me?

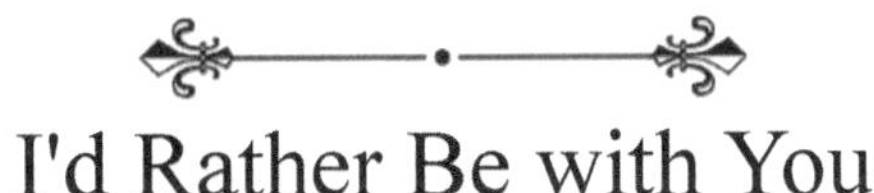

I'd Rather Be with You

We laugh with love
We bond with joy
Each and every celebration
Yet I'd rather be with you
Even in tears
Filling up my empty heart

We cheer our hearts out
We come together as one
Over meaningless games we give meaning too
Yet I'd rather see you at your worst frown
And mayhaps bring out that million-dollar smile
That warms the air surrounding you

We feast to celebrate
Foods loaded with taste
Fill our bellies to the barrel
Yet your eyes are my desire
Even if they are heavy with sorrow
They still glimmer with your ceaseless hope

We play all day
Hours of swear toil and fun
For the rights to reign victorious
Yet I'd rather hear that angelic voice
Even if it's all choked up
It rings as heavenly as mortals may

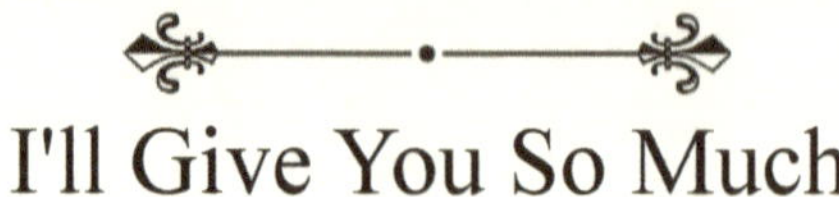

I'll Give You So Much

I'll give you my time until you get bored with me
I'll give you my jokes until you get tired of them
I'll give you my assistance until I can't help you

My commitment my loyalty until time stops
My heart my mind until the worms eat it
My depth of soul from my soul will light you up and give you meaning
and depth until you're a different person from all the love
My words of comfort and cheer until you can't smile
My gifts of chocolates and foods I'll cook/bake you until your stuffed
My gifs of flowers with meaning and purpose so I can say every time
"but they're not as beautiful as you;)" until your last breath
My gifts of events going places visiting new areas exploring until
we've seen it all
My gift (God's gift?) of walks… is it just me or is there no better time
to talk to those you love than on a walk? I'd go everyday with you if
you'd let me until you can't
My gifts of poetry and writing…. I'll try to write you good ones….
until you get annoyed with them
My money to spend as you see fit cause I trust you with all of it to be
responsible…. until you don't need or want anything anymore

I Give You All of Me

My legs for walking with
My arms for hugs
My lips for kissing
My mouth for conversation
My funny bone for jokes;)
My ankles for flexibility
My elbows for space for just us two
My hands for touching you creating ecstasy
My feet for dance (I wanna learn to slow dance just for you)
My shoulders to cry on
My waist for comfort
My gut for all the punches of frustrations
My fingers for poetry
My head to rule as a servant leader
My mind as a wonderland waiting for you to explore it
My eyes so you have a man to look good for
My ears to listen to you about anything
My heart to match the beauty of yours

So It Was Me

All alone
I had some friends
But not that friend
That one of a kind
Only room for one of her
Kinda friend
The irreplaceable
I still haven't found you
But I feel a connection
Between two souls in perfect harmony
A bond deeper than brother
Call me a dreamer
But not even dreamers
Reach the level of love we will

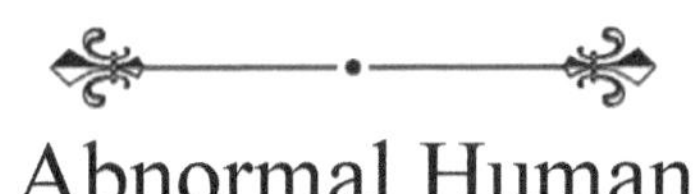

Abnormal Human

I talked to Superman
He didn't understand me
He thought he did
But deep down…he was flawless
I asked him if he understood pain
He said of course he has
He felt the pain of loss and violence

But the pain of being human no
The pain of being limited
Of not knowing the answer
Of not being able to save
Of letting down your greatest ally
The pain of not being able to thrive
Not being able to provide
Not being good enough
Not an abled communicator
And he asked me
would you like to trade places for a day?

I said no
I like the pain of humanity
It brings out the best in us
I believe that God Is Almighty
That anything made can be unmade
That any damage can be healed
That any sorrow can be turned to joy

I believe that the man is made in the image of God
That he can create like Him
Have morality like Him
And serve like Him
I believe that God is good

That He is by nature the morality we strive for
That He holds the wisdom we strive for
That He gives mankind purpose
Being a beacon of light to ideal towards

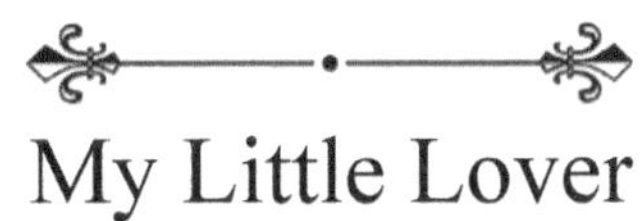

My Little Lover

My woman
I'll probably go thru phases
Of not treating you as I should
Of my mind wandering
But at my core I will always have you above me
I can always write you poetry
Buy you flowers
Do the dishes for you
Whatever it takes
To keep you

My lover
There will be times
Times of challenge
And un-romanticness from me
But in my heart, you'll always be my one and only
But I can fix it
Give me the word
I'll take you out
Dress up fancy to match you
Show you that I never forgot you

My best friend
I may get boring to you
You may get boring to me
But my heart is loyal
I will always love you
We can spruce things up
Turn things back
To recreate that magic
Do things to reinvigorate our relationship
Because you have the depth and intrigue
To keep me glued to your wonderland forever

Sojourner

I came from a distant land
New to the area
And found friends
But they forgot me
Like a play tool from childhood

I embraced them
I loved them
We bonded
But in the end
I was just another crashing wave

Did I leave a mark?
Graffiti at least?
No but I left
An empty chair
Proving I came and went

All Roads Lead to Love

Millions of ways to show you I love you
Flowers for your beauty
Jewels for your elegance
Chocolates for your sweetness
Not just on Valentine's Day
Different ways of language to communicate
I can write poetry
I can speak eloquently
I can use metaphors and similes
To say the same three words

Alternate routes of creativity show
By going on walks
By taking you on dates
By listening and comprehending
Everything all accumulates
To
I
Love
You

You Give Me Meaning Reason and Purpose

I wanna give you a reason
A reason to look good
A reason to stay slim
A reason to fancy your hair

That the depths of my soul can
Reach out through my eyes
And witness true beauty

I wanna give you purpose
Purpose to be merciful
Purpose to be virtuous
Purpose to have character

Because deep down in your soul
That beautiful soul
Enhances my love you for you

I wanna give you meaning
Meaning to be a lover
Meaning to be a mother
Meaning to be holy

Because everything you are
Is a perfect counter-piece to mine
And reflects our belief set
That we are only as great
And me and you together

Because your beauty
Reflects the inward parts
And inspires me to be better
Because your inward beauty

Captivates me to the point
I want no other

Because without you
Me means nothing
And my soul would wander
Seeking meaning purpose reason
Forever unquenched
Without you

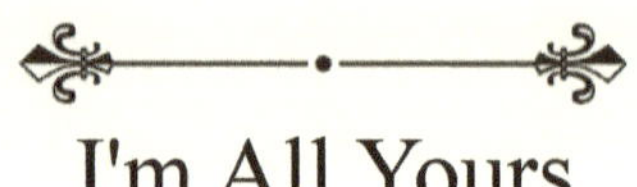

I'm All Yours

If I had no one else
No other girl
For fear of my girl
Hehe amen sister

I wouldn't have it
Any other way
If women were terrified
Of flirting with me
For fear of the wrath
Of my women
Hehe amen woman
I wouldn't have it
Any other way

If women
Never approached me
Because they knew about
My woman
I'd wear the biggest
Goofiest ring to repel them
Just so they knew
I'm a one-woman kinda man

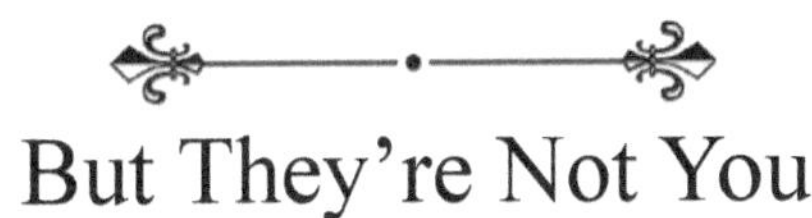

But They're Not You

I could date other women
The most beautiful
Elegance and poise
Sexy and pure
But it wouldn't be you
So, I wouldn't care

I could talk to other women
The funniest
Best conversations
Most interesting
But it wouldn't be the same
So, I wouldn't care

I could find the purest
The holiest women
Who beliefs perfectly align
And teach me truths
But I'd still want you
So, I'd wait for you

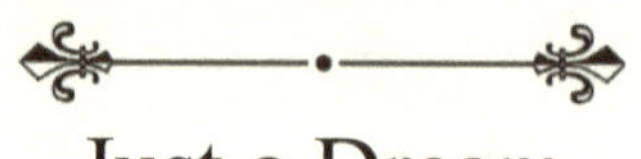

Just a Dream

I dreamt her up
Said she was real
Said if I can dream it
God musta already made it
Impossible they say
No one is perfect for another
I kept writing her
I kept believing
But at some point
I gotta give up
Don't I?

What am I holding on to?
I want her to be real
But dreaming ain't reality
And I've gone too far
Maybe I'll love a normal wife
Nothing special nothing great
Just another brick in the wall

Depression 101

Life seems so futile
So empty
So meaningless
I do things
I'm with people
But all I wanna do is sleep

I could write about
The depth of God
Loving your neighbor
Making a difference for others
But there are times
I just don't care

There are times
I wanna live
And do and create
Yet even with her
I think I'd still feel meaningless
This pain just comes and goes

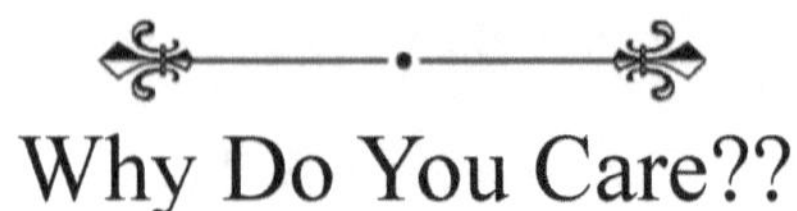

Why Do You Care??

I asked why
Why did people
Care about me?
I waited
Best I got was
You're like me

I asked how
How could they
Remember me?
I was a nobody
They said its cause
They were too

I asked when
When could I see
Their faces and hear the
Their voices
They reminded me
Eternities a long time

My Fantasy

I said I wanted her
A perfect soulmate
One of a kind
Made for me
Like my heart
Fantasy, they said
But even the fantasy
Drives me wild
And lights this soul afire

I wrote out what I wanted
A gem beyond compare
Better than any seen before
Full of character virtue and truth
Smart heartfelt and full of life
The desire of any and all men
The envy of other women
I didn't think I was good worthy
But that high made me alive

I could doubt
I could settle
But my heart agrees with my mind
My soul aligns with my fantasy
She is the epitome of perfect
My one and only
I will love you and only you
Redefining love into something higher
Making fantasy reality

Impossible

They said finding love like I want is impossible
They also said man flying was
They said my dream of a perfect woman is a fantasy
They also said cloning was fantasy
They said the idea of us being made for each other was fiction
They also said reaching mars was fiction
They said it's not realistic to expect so much and give so much
They also said that leaving the earth wasn't either
They said two lovers couldn't be together forever
I said God stayed true for thousands of years… why no us?
They said it's you imagining your love
I said all imagination is based off reality
They said it'll never work
I said mankind was made to make the impossible possible
They said she's not real
You wouldn't think someone like me existed either would you?
They say the perfect romance is a lie
They've lied about everything else… why not this?

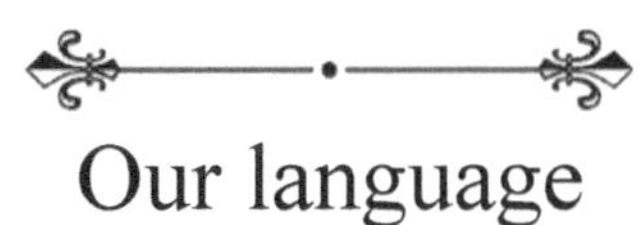

Our language

I wrote to her
I develop a language
I conveyed my love
But I never asked
Does she love me?

I wanted her so bad
I thought about her
Constantly
She was all I cared about
But I never thought
Am I what's best for her?

I felt pain without her
But I never experienced
The hells of pain she went through
Please forgive me woman
How can I repay you?
Or make it up to you??

I'm sorry I'm so selfish
And only push my desire
Of you for myself
I don't know if you want me
If am best for you
Or if I can take away the pain
I just don't wanna let you down

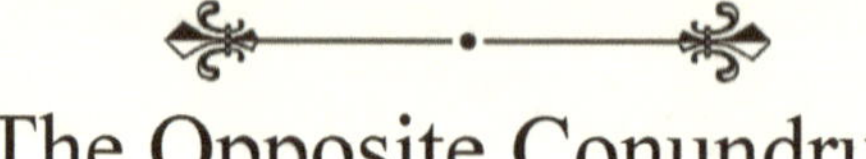

The Opposite Conundrum

I wanted happiness
But without enough sorrow
I couldn't reach the heights I wanted
Not without intense letdown

I wanted strength
But without enough pain
I couldn't obtain the power I wanted
Theres a tradeoff for all desires

I wanted wisdom
But I was afraid to play the fool
Little did I realize
The wise gain from foolish questions

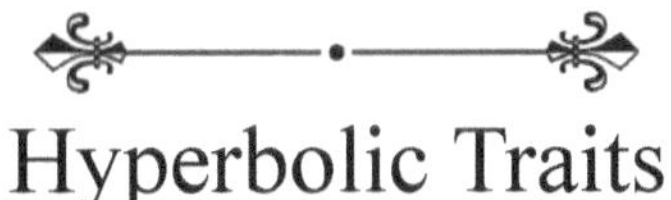

Hyperbolic Traits

Too serious and you're a stickler
Too much humor and you're a joke
Too kind and you're a pushover
Too harsh and your cruel
Too embracing and your clingy
Too distant and your cold
Too smart and you're a nerd
Too dumb and you're a fool
Too innocent and your inexperienced
Too guilty and you're a pariah
Too strong and you're a meathead
Too weak and you're a sissy
Too social you don't find yourself
Too antisocial you don't meet others
Too dedicated you become a fanatic
Too indifferent nothing matters to you
Too much shallow you can't relate
Too much depth no one understands you

Time space and matter

How do we function without time?
What is creation without change?
If we stand stuck in time
We just are for a time
Nothing different nothing forward
We can't be for more than that moment
Time is what makes life possible

How do we function without space?
What is time without space?
And where would time be?
If we can't go from one space
To another what are we?
We can't live or move or grow or act…
We're just shadows

How do we function without matter?
What good are time and space with matter?
Existing in a body with possibility
The ability to move to think to emote
To react and interact and just plain act
All culminating in our being
A body and mind completes us

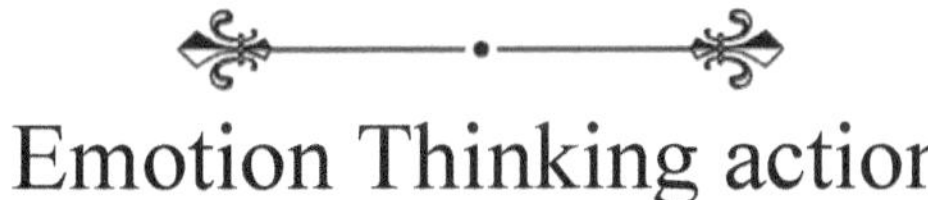

Emotion Thinking action

We feel
Our first ability
We cry cause were afraid
We smile for joy experience
Even babies emote feelings
Before complex (thought or action)
We feel intensely

We act
In every way anyway we can
We test the limits of mankind
We experience life
Through what we do
Use our senses to accumulate
All around us so we can
Replicate our greatness with action

We think
The deepest of these
The philosophical proof of life
Trumps actions done
As it puts them into motion
And rivals' emotion
To see which is more substantial
But leads us deeper
As it explains emotions and actions

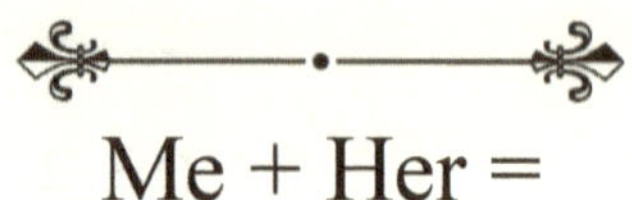

Me + Her =

As sparks plus wood creates fire
So, me and her together is lit

As hydrogen and oxygen combine to be water
So, me plus her is essential chemistry

As the sky and electricity show lightning
So, my love and her depth allow wonder

As man gives nature meaning
So does she create purpose within me

As a king rules alongside his queen
So do I need her by me as a councilor

As two inseparable friends mourn apart
So too does my soul feel pain without you

Like a dog in depression without its master
So, I wait emptily to see that glorious face

As men and women compliment
So were me and made for each other

As time needs space and matter needs both
So does she complete me to the depths of my soul

As actions give words meaning
So too does her reciprocation of my love make it worthwhile

You Outdid 'Em All

If someone was more physically beautiful
I'd feel sorry for her man
Cause she ain't as beautiful a soul as yours

If someone was sexier
I wouldn't care
Cause you have so much heart

If someone was more fun to be around
I'd say that's impossible
There's no one I'd rather spend time with

If I could be everywhere at once
And date every woman at the same time
I'd get bored with them
And have 7 billion versions of me
Serving you and vying for your attention

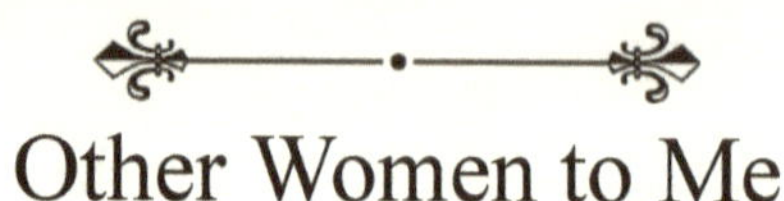

Other Women to Me

I see other women
Women with virtue
Women that believe the truth
Women of grace and compassion
But they're not you

I remember you love
I remember your faithfulness
I remember your flawless soul
I remember you, all of you
And I cry in my mind
Forever thinking of other women

I want you to be mine alone
So, I should be yours alone
I want to be one with you
Without any distractions
I want you to understand my love
the depth the passion the loyalty
So, I don't wanna share it with another

My Redhead

Those long flowing locks of red
Shining forth in brilliance
Almost making the rest of her invisible
Radiating like a precious ruby
But it means so much more than appearance
It keeps your eyes fixated
Deceiving you as if it's just for looks
But the color has depth to it
Some say redheads are crazy
But each has their own craze
Mine is… in the best way
She's crazy… about God
She's crazy about truth
About justice and mercy
Always willing to suffer for what's right
Never able to succumb to fear
A warrior of flaming red light

Red

Red
The color of passion
Intensity at its finest
Making everything mean more
The depth of caring doesn't waver

Red
The color of devotion
Dedication to the purest of intentions
The most loyal and faithful
Never leaving under any circumstance

Red
The color of beauty
So deep is heaps to the fabric of my soul
So pure it can't be stained
Unlimited in power and appearance

Red
The color of love
Making things matter because they care
Passionately dedicated
Devoted beyond measure
Beauty beyond fathoming

Red
Her color
My dream
My woman
My love
My heaven

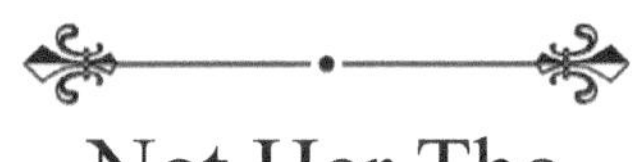

Not Her Tho

I'm kind to others
But not the depth of kindness I have for her
I'll tease her if it makes her laugh
Hug her if she wants to cry
And serve her as my queen
I care about others
But not to the depth of care I have for her
I'll spend time with her
Comfort her when she's down
My mind focused on her and how to make her feel special

I love others
But not the depth of passion I love her
She's my one and only woman
I'll do things for her id do for no one else
I'll sacrifice my life to make hers a dream

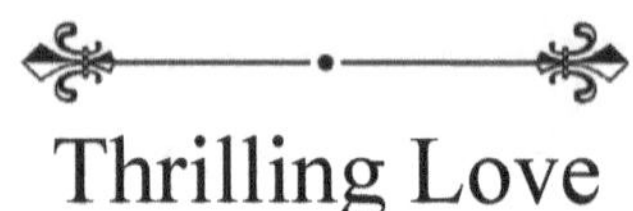

Thrilling Love

If I was a superhero
Saving the day
Punishing villains
The most thrilling adventure
Would be my life with her

If I was a leader
Saving the country from corruption
Fighting against the fifth
Fighting for the people
The most fulfilling events in my life
Would be my time with her

If I was wealthy
The richest man on earth
I'd spend my fortune on her
To make her happy
To satisfy her desires
But even so
The money would mean nothing
Without her

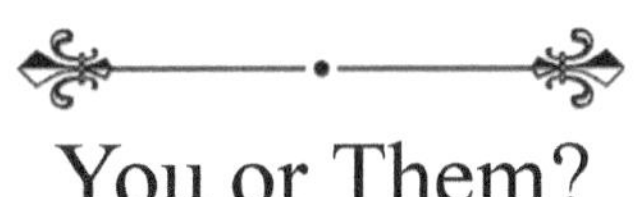

You or Them?

What matters more wellbeing or relationships
What matters more your health or the health of your loved
ones…
what's more painful you dying or a loved one…
What brings more joy… your smile or a loved one

Everyman Dies...

What does it mean to live?
To really live??
We all die
But do we all experience life to the fullest?
Is it our relationships with others?

Maybe having a lot of friends?
Or having a deep personal friend?
Or raising a family?
Is it seeking truth?
Separating fact from fiction?
Seeking for the honest happenings?
Or searching for new light?

Maybe the answer lies in morality
Living by doing what's right?
By abiding by the highest standard?
And being dedicated to a life of value?
Or maybe Christianity is right?
Have a relationship with Christ... the best friend
Seek after the truth of the Bible … the way to heaven
Live after the morality of faith… the way of submission to righteousness
If there is a Creator… His way is life…for He created life

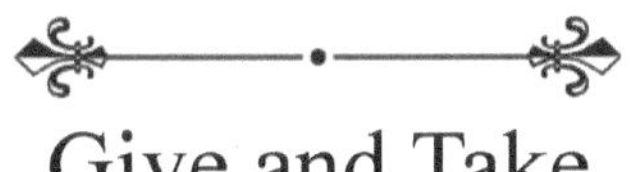

Give and Take

Without listening there would be no reason to talk
Silence makes the noise possible
Solitude and pain are a bad combination
Solutions are solved patterns
Virtue is the chief principle separating man and beast
Work is a blessing … those who never work never know what they are capable of
The greatest blessings come with the smallest hearts
Those filled with hate often despise themselves
You'll never know what you can't do until you give up
You'll find your will is stronger when you care more about someone
(Maybe that's why Gods will is so powerful… He cares immensely for all His creation)
Always remember: God vehemently hates sending anyone to hell, even the most egregious sinner... it goes against His will

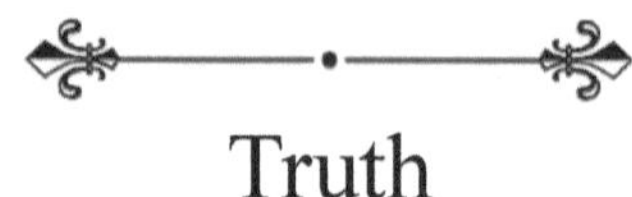

Truth

What is want
But a desire for more in life
What is passion
But your heart craving uncontrollable for that one love
What is heartache
But the soul telling the mind its hurting
What is eureka
But the mind making sense of the unpattern
What is clarity
But seeing like light in darkness
What is carnage
But good people allowing the evil to rule
What is prosperity
But the little ones growing up in peace purity and order
What is genius
But pattern recognition that no one else saw
What is fortitude
But forging ahead in the worst of times
What is forgiveness
But laying aside their just deserts in mercy
What is horror
But losing the love of your life
What is repentance
But a way to change who you were
What is time
But a path where you can only go forward
What Is music
But a way to express emotion
What is life
But a chance to prove your love
What is death
But a dénouement

Sweet Lasting Lady

I love you so much woman….
If I ever disappoint you let me know
My soul mate was glorious
Everyone wanted her
Shining forth brightly
As a divine being

I looked in the mirror
I saw bald
I saw the limitations I had
I didn't think I Was worthy
I heard her voice
Softly through the wind
You belong to me

I see your worth inside
I know your troubles
Your trials your pains
And I want you more
More than any other
Because you were made for me
And I for you

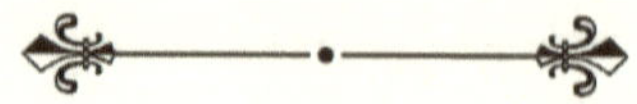

Mercy Forgiveness and Compassion Belong to These

Mercy is the virtue
Of righteous victors
Because they hate war
And despise the bloodshed

Forgiveness is the virtue
Of the Godly
As God forgave man
Man forgives his fellow trespasser

Compassion is the virtue
Of the manly and strong
Because you can't have compassion
On one stronger than you

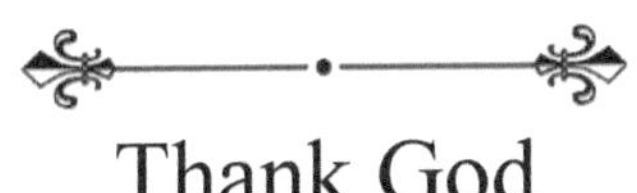

Thank God

Thank you God
For giving me your favorite
I don't care if she wasn't…
She is now
At least she's mine

Thank you, God, for entrusting me
With her depth her character
And her virtue that never ends
Help me to live up to her

Thank you, God, for gifting me
With the most priceless treasure
Mankind can receive
A perfect match to complement me
Thank you, God, for making her
The better half of me
The more beautiful part
And the biggest reason I love you

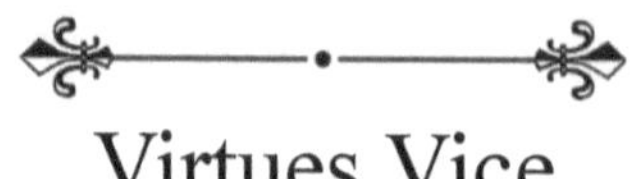

Virtues Vice

What good is virtue
If there was never vice in the world?
What good I character
Without tests?
What good is morality
If there were no immorality?
What good is mercy
If we couldn't annihilate?
What good is compassion
With looking the other way?
What good is time
If we can't change?
What good is music
If you can't hear?
What good is repentance
If you revert back?
What good is a man's word
If he can't be honest?
What good is challenge
If you can never lose?
What good is destruction
If you can build back?
What good is power
Without people to rule over?
What good is genius
If we all knew everything?
What good is love
If it doesn't last forever?
What good is wisdom
If no one understands it?
What good is wisdom
When no one comprehends it?
Why do you seek for more understanding

If you can't share it with another??
What good are breakthroughs
If you don't explain their use?
When you're the only one it affects
Does it even matter?
What good is life
Without another to share it with?
A friend a relative a lover?
All alone what are you?
If you don't connect with others?
If you don't transfer something to another
If you live to yourself and yourself alone
Are you even human?
WHAT GOOD IS GOD WITHOUT CREATION???if you ever feel low… remember this… you give God meaning

A Woman That Doesn't Lie?!?

If you said my woman lied
I'd say you were the liar-
She doesn't lie and
Vehemently hates liars

If you accused my woman
Of being unfaithful
I'd say you've got the wrong woman
My women loves me too much

If you accused my woman
Of mistreating anyone
I'd say that's impossible
She has a heart of gold
And holds no ill will

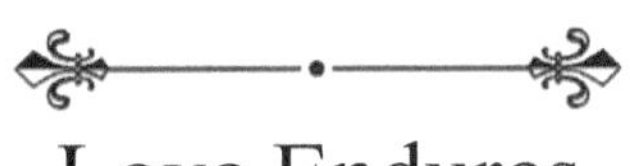

Love Endures

Nations will rise
Empires will fall
The fate of the world
Will hang in the brink
But my love will be steady

The earth will die
Everything living thing gone
Nothing left to inhabit
No more human race
But my love with linger

I will come into your life
I will love you with everything
I will pass away
Gone from your life
But my love will be with you

My love will eternally scream
"I was always there for in life
I will be there in death
I will cry out to God to give you His
greatest angels to comfort and protect you."

And when you feel alone without me
Close your eyes
And remember my words
The same words of God
"I am always with you
I will never leave nor forsake you
I love you with an everlasting love"
And if my love Is everlasting
So are we

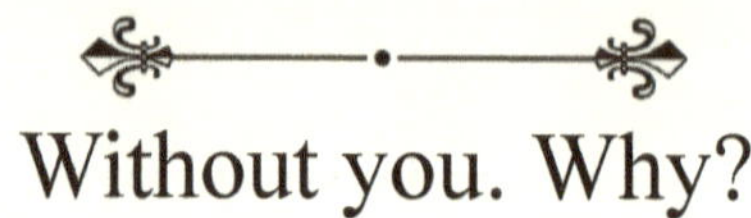

Without you. Why?

Why would I wanna be President
When can be the luckiest
More blest than them
By being with you

Why would I desire riches
Other than to give to you (to see you smile)
All the money Is rubbish without you
When you're the greatest prize

Why would I give up
My friend's family
Free time freedom
If not for that soul
That finally makes me feel
Alive and worthwhile

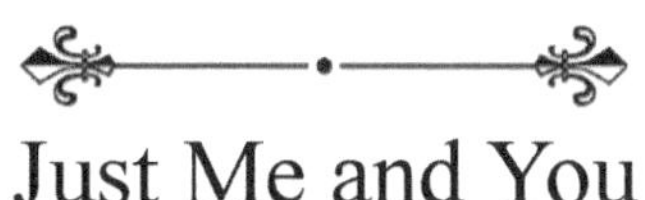

Just Me and You

They want you
But never me
I want you
Only

Why is it?
That the hand that asks
Never gives
Why Is it?

I desire you
Always
Forever
But without them

Lost and Return

When no one can help?
I seek God
When God is hidden?
I seek my lover

My love where is the pain?
I can wash that sting away
My love where is the loss?
I can find you a path back to the Creator

I have enemies all around
Yet no one to comfort her
The Invisible remains
And so, does she
Thus despair
Yet In time...
The invisible will return
God will comfort greater
And I will glorify His name above all

Special Kinda Woman

I killed myself internally because life without her was useless
I emptied myself of pleasure cause pleasure without was impossible
I carried forth without sanity because she was the sanity to my unhinged mindset
will I ever come to my senses and understand: can woman love? The way men can?

I sought her with diligence because I needed an escape
I drove off the map cause I was lost
I wanted her to save me cause I was irredeemable
yet I realized something: you can't be what isn't yours to become!

I loved that she wasn't like the rest because the rest were empty followers
I loved that she was the manliest women ever because I was afraid no women would understand me
I loved that she was the purest innocent beautiful girly girl ever because I was the darkest monster I knew And I came to know that the only pain worse than pain itself is living without her

What is This Life?

I was human
A soul floating in a body
A mind looking through the eyes
A heart pumping out energy
Then I evolved

I lost my empathy
Gained intuition
Lost my emotion
Gained a cerebral mindset
And despised humanity

A human came
And reasoned
Why evolve?
But to reach down to the lowest
And empathize

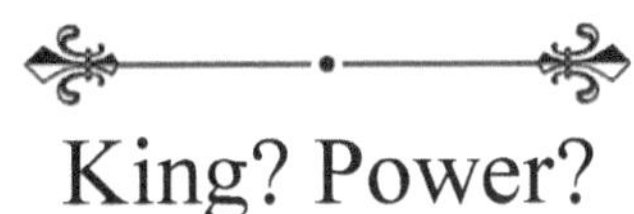

King? Power?

The tiger clenched its fists in rage
The bird escaped
The wind escaped the field
And all the tiger did
Was stare

The tiger prowled for its prey
The antelope fled
The grass escaped the meat
And all the tiger did
Was stare

The tiger sought for dominance
And his dominion was taken
The bird the antelope and others
And all the tiger did
Was ponder

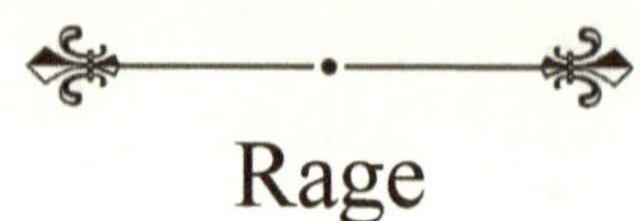

Rage

Fist of rage
Rage
Heart of rage
Rage
Bloody rage
Rage
Knuckles of rage
Rage
Mind of rage
Rage
Soul of rage
Rage
Peace of rage
Rage
Virtue of rage
Rage
Fortune of rage
Rage
March of rage
Rage
Violence of rage
Rage
End of rage
Rage
Rage never ends
In the hearts of the restless abandon and lost

What Have We Become?

Together we left it all
Together we spat in the face of society
Together we looked down at the worms
Sitting above after years below

We trod the low life
We earned our spot up high
We sought for so much more
Perched as a vulture circling

The end Is nigh
The end is a higher plane
But you and me
We made it there already

The Worst of Us

Birds chatter
Prairie dogs chirp
Yet your voice
Is like the worm

Dogs cuddle
cats cradle
And you my dear
Spike like a porcupine

Fish swim
Eagles fly
Yet you
Can't walk the walk of a man

Beyond the Imagination

Futile
The life
The planet
The solar system
Yet above all
The mind

Forsaken
My home
My country
My kindred
But above all
The soul

Foreshadowed
The prophesy
The whisper
The promise
But not
My death
Home
My death is still in tune
Escape is futile
Time space is pulling
And me
I belong there

Back Foul Beast

People crawl to me like worms
Asking what is life
I say a worm's life is dirt
They say I am no worm
I say wipe that smudge

People fly at me like bugs
Asking what is death
I saw annihilation
They don't get that one step
Is death

People come at me like a tiger
Trying to terrify me with horror
But they don't understand
The hunter hunts with a shotgun
And explains that life and death
Comes at the hands of man

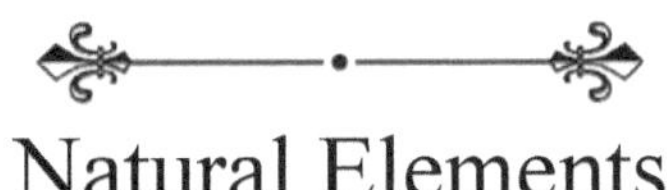

Natural Elements

Echoes
Coming before the sound
Blinding my ears with noise
Telling me I'll never succeed
Because I'm just an echo

Light
Coming before the tunnel
Stopping at matter
While time stands still
Screeching me to a halt before the journey starts

Gravity
Pulling me towards the sky
Showing me that I don't belong on this earth
That all life is a drag
And that the air was made to uplift you

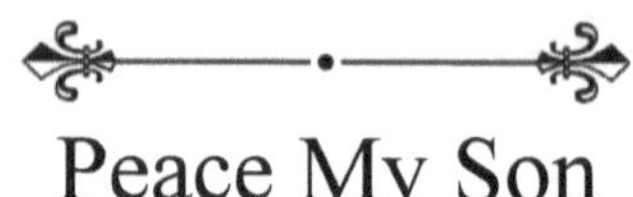

Peace My Son

Savage repercussions come unawares
We rage against our superior inferiors and codependents
But little do we think of ourselves as synergy
Coming together as a whole

We consolidate in our trifles
Yet never a dilution comes where peace confirms virtue
Setting ourselves up for disappointing success
Never-ending yearning for the pain's loss

Painstaking turmoil ends the cycle
The cycle of never-ending prosperous greed
Which none compete with and all succumb too
Heavenly blessing let us rest

Transcendence

Squares shape into the third dimension
Transcending time and space
While we stay behind in one conscious
Oblivious to the world that could be

What if we as people could pause time?
To see the world as it were without haste
Never-ending never ceasing notwithstanding
What if we saw the innocence of life and could
Just for one second smile

The last to go is the first to stay
Because we never leave the heroes behind
Crying wolf won't solve your problems
But standing up to internal fears will

The Opposite of Peace

Synergy completes the matrix
Cycling through the masters will
Breaking free of cowardice and mistrust
We stand afoot on victories hill

Cynicism destroys the willpower
Diabolic plans leave behind
No one falls obliged to fire
Passion fades within the well

Fortunes favors those who falter
As the heroes indue the service to their spouses
Crying to hear the voice of a martyr we lift our minds in solidarity
For the unforgettable

Black was the darkness
Covered in heaviness
Layered in depth
Dark as the night

In the night we fearmongered
In the darkness we holistically approached our fears
Edging farther from realty
We expressed our greatest fear:
Chaos

EVA

Eva
We never met
But we will
Because I and you are we

Eva
They don't believe
In us
But one day they'll see

Eva
He was wrong
They are
But I'm not

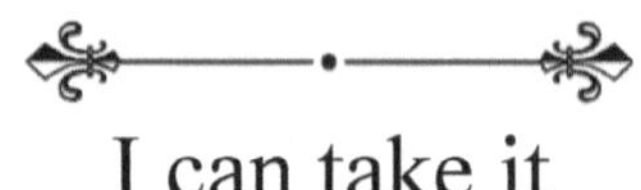

I can take it

Dear woman…
If you hate me
I can take your hate
Please lash out at me if need be
I'll take you punches
But in the end
I know you'll come to your senses
Cause I always love you
Even in your hate

If you disagree with me
Let me know
Use facts and logic
Maybe I'm wrong
We'll hash it out
Until we can reach
A place that settles
So, we both can see truth
Cause I'll be able to see past minor obsessions
As I respect your intelligence

If you get angry
That's okay
I'll be a tank for myself
That can take your animosity
But a punching bag for you
To take all that frustration
I'm strong woman
I can take your emotions
Just come back one day
And receive my love
If you lose it
And despise me as anything worse than your Man

It's okay. I'll forgive you
I'm not in this for power

I want power to protect you and comfort you
I'm not in it to rule over you with a rod
I wanna rule over you to give you freedom
And blessings and elevate you
As my partner

I don't ever wanna hurt you
But I'm human
So, forgive me ahead of time
But what I'm trying to say is
I can take your abuse and obscenities
Because I know it's not your nature
I know you have a beautiful soul
That wouldn't wanna hurt me
But we are all human
And even if you slip
I won't hold grudges
That's not who I am

I wanna take in your frustrations
And flip them around to positive vibes
Right back at you
Woman what do you think of me?????
Cause I think the world of you…

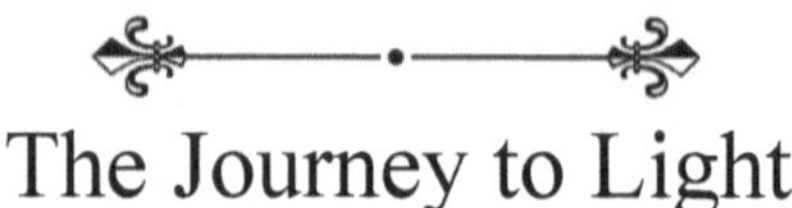

The Journey to Light

I faltered
But a hand was there to pick me up

I fell hard
But grace come over me to rise up again

I misspoke
But the truth was spoken to wash me clean

I hated
But one showed me forgiveness
So, I followed

I got lost
But my guide showed me the way home

I disobeyed
But my teacher corrected me
And I amended my ways

I gave up
It was too much to bear
I didn't wanna fight anymore

But I heard a voice from the future
Pleading with me
To continue on

So, I disobeyed my spirit
And followed the voice
And with a heart of gratitude
I stood

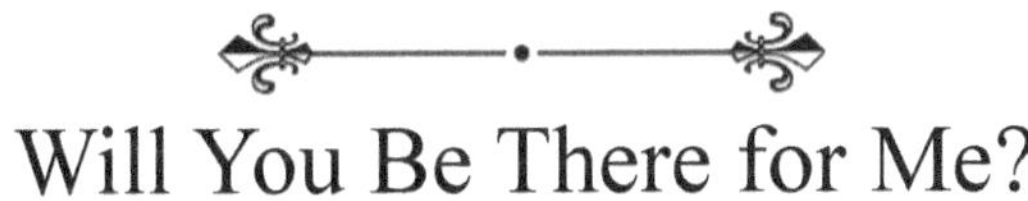

Will You Be There for Me?

I'm thankful for her loyalty
That she would never leave me

I'm thankful for her character
That shines like a star

I'm Thankful for her beauty
For hidden and revealed

I'm Thankful for our future friendship
That we may grow together as one

I'm Thankful for her grace
Her forgiveness and mercy

I'm thankful that she chose me
Outta all the men in the world
I belong to her and her alone

I'm thankful for her love
I can feel it dear woman,
It pushes me forward
Towards you

I'm thankful for words
So, I can express my love for you
I'm Thankful for actions
So, I can prove my love for you

I'm thankful you're out there
And have patience for me
I'm thankful you exist
So that when nothing makes sense

I have one woman out there
That reciprocates my love
I'm thankful that we can grow old together
And remember in the future the presents past

I'm thankful for the amazing children you will give me
That I may have a line of successors
To carry on my work

I'm thankful everyday
Is one day closer
To use meeting for the first time
And spending the rest of our lives
As one

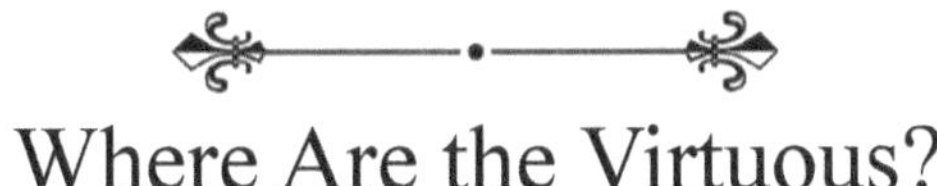

Where Are the Virtuous?

Where is the man of faith?
Pleading with the evil to amend their ways
Preaching the way of peace and charity
Leading people to all truth?
They've turned and went their own way

Where Is the man of strength?
Conquering his own demons
Battling fierce corruption
Lighting burdens of others outta brotherhood
They seek their own power

Where is the man of justice
Out to serve and protect the meek
And out the wicked corrupt men of per in their places
Watching out for the little man with no guardian
They sold out for silver

Where is the man of mercy?
Ending generations of revenge
Seeking unity among the righteous
Seeking goodwill and compassion on all
They've been corrupted and twisted

Where is the man of courage?
Taking a firm stance for all that is right in the world
Debating corrupt evil doers without shame
Fighting for those who have no voice
They threw the towel in after all the attacks

Where is the man of humility?
Putting others needs above his watch
Pleading for aid so he can be the best he can be
Obeying the laws of all that is good without praise
He's been conquered, no good man is left

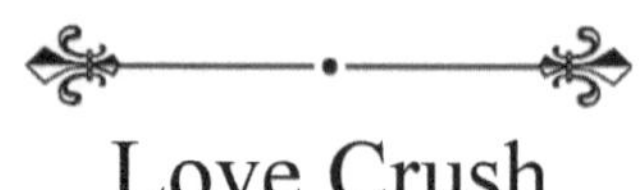

Love Crush

O desire of my heart
I long for you as the earth longs for the sun
As the tides connect to the moon
My heart is intertwined with yours
What does it take to see you???

Love of my life
My passion burns as a volcano
My soul erupts with bliss at the thought of you
You are the key to my happiness (forgive me)
When will I be able to show you?

O dearest woman
The only one I want
All others seem like trophies
But you seem like a living soul
When can I experience the marvels that we create
Together?

Oh, beauty that extends beyond physical matter
I've looked for you as a blind man looks for light
Knowing not where to search
Knowing not what it's like to see true beauty
Hoping that can set me free
And show me what it looks like
To find love everlasting…

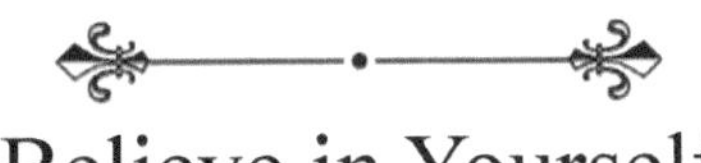

Believe in Yourself

When you think you're not good enough
Remember I've been waiting my whole life for you
Praying and pleading for you
Always searching diligently
Remember: you belong to me

When you think you're not pretty enough
Let me tell you something
Beauty starts form the soul
And transcends basic looks
What good is looks without heart?

When you think you're not worthy
Who, in reality, is worthy?
We all fail, fall short
It's those who learn from that
And learn to pick themselves up
And in reality, I don't feel worthy of you…

If you're ever nervous…
You're alive with nerves
Its part of being human
Just realize the worst you've done
Can be forgiven
And those who mock you
Are ants

If your ever scared
It's part of life
A self-protection mechanism
Realize that even the fiercest
Beast experiences fear
So maybe that's you

The fiercest beast;)

If you ever worried
Let your cares flow like water
You have such little control
Over this or that
Assume the best
And when the worst happens
You won't be worried
You'll face your fear head on

KNOW

If you're rejected
Know you belong to me
If you're confused…
Know I will enlighten

If you're in sorrow
Know we'll weep together
If you're lost
Know well find a path together

If you don't know…
Know I love your honesty
If you are feeling small
Know I love your humility

If you're wanting
Know ill give you all I've got
If you're feeling alone
Know I'm with you in spirit

If you are alive
Know I will always cherish you
If you are mine
Know you will always be
If you are unloved
Know the whole world will be jealous
Of my love for you

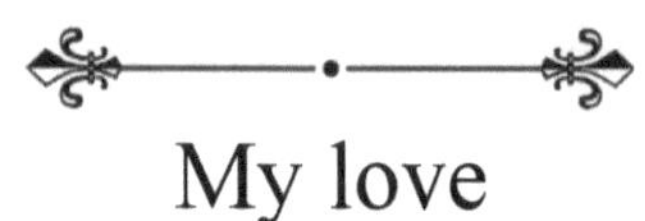

My love

My love
Will outlast time
And transcend space

My love
Will make time stop
And never cease

My love
Will ease your pain
To the point of ecstasy

My love
Will fill the empty air
And surround you in comfort

My love
Will cease your doubts
And bring clarity

My love
Will end your searching
and will guide you

My love
Will surpass you best dreams
And eliminate any nightmare

My love
Will be there in sorrow
And ease your troubled mind

My love

Will remind you I'm enough
And make all your past forgotten

My love
Will make others' mundane
And excite that beautiful mind

My love
Will make you forget
All that came before

My love
Will continue after death
And always comfort you
My love
Will replace what was
And set joy inside
Forever

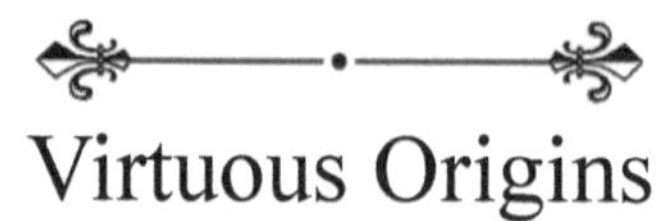

Virtuous Origins

The highs of joy
Began when I understood sorrow

The depth of peace
Began after great confusion

The sounds of laughter
Began after rivers of tears

The mountains of faith I moved
Began after years of doubt

The strength others admire
Began with endless failures

The courage to take a stand
Began after countless fears

The wisdom of sages
Began with unlimited questions

The hope for tomorrow
Began with a hopeless past

Peace of mind
Began with struggles of demons

And the love of God
Began with hatred for the Almighty
But ended with blissful love
Eternal

What is Failure? What is Success?

Failure is
When you don't take the shot
Success is
When you give it everything
Failure is
When. you don't show up
Success is
When your dedicated to your craft
Failure is
When you look down at a struggling fighter
Success is
When you respect the underdog
Failure is
When you think your too good
Success is
When you go out there and annihilate them
Failure is
When you seek not understanding
Success is
When you the desire to learn
Failure is
When you don't learn from your mistakes
Success is
When you grow as a human from your experiences
Failure is
When you mock the weak and lowly
Success is
When you have compassion on them
Failure is
When you give up from hardship
Success is
When you take the pain and keep going
Failure is

Selling your soul for power
Success is
Grinding as a beacon of light
Failure is loving money more than people
Success is
Mercy on your fellow man
Failure is
Walking with anyone who gets you places
Success is
Willing to walk alone to do what's right

At the End of the Day… What Have You Done for God???

Being friends with a brother is great
Being friends with God is superior
Having love for your woman is great
Having love for God Is superior
Being good to the poor is great
Being good to God is superior
Being loyal to your wife is great
Being loyal to God is superior
Being dedicated to family is great
Being dedicated to God is superior
Being a hero of mankind is great
Being a hero if the faith is superior
Being a man of wisdom is great
Being a man of the wisdom of the Bible superior
Dedicating your life to religion is great
Dedicating your life to God is superior
Suffering for good is great
Suffering for God is superior
Dying for a cause is great
Dying for God is superior
Only one could help

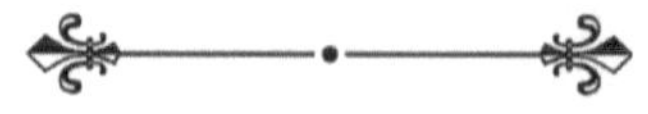

He Was Always There for Me

I cried
No one heard
No one cared
Each to His own
But God heard
God Cared
And God wept with me

I feel into the valley of the show of death
People mocked me
People made it more dangerous
People thought I got what I deserved
But God cared
And God protected me

All I heard was a million different lucifers
In every way taking me from my God
All enticing me to go everywhere but to God
God ended it, despised it, and set me free
Because God loves me
Forgive me Lord

Accountability

We lost
It was his fault
No, his
Everyone's fault
But mine

We won
It was a little bit your win
A little bit his
We all played a hand
But it wasn't their fault they lost

I erred
When I blame others
Nothing good happens
But when I take it personal
Confess my sins
And amend my ways
Magic happens
And people forgive

My Nature Was Corrupt

I could blame the world
Blame my upbringing
My culture
But none of that solves anything
But when I take a deep look at myself
I see the only way to change something
Is to assess myself with honesty
To take the steps necessary to change
Seek the heavens for help
And rise above

On the Twelve Days of my Lovers Christmas

On the first day of Christmas my soul mate gave me…
Her heart of gold
On the second day of Christmas my soul mate gave me…
Her devotion to me
On the third day of Christmas my soul mate gave to me…
Her time
On the fourth day of Christmas my soul mate gave to me…
Her love and affection
On the fifth day of Christmas my soul mate gave to me …
The gift of friendship
On the sixth day of Christmas my soul mate gave to me…
Brilliant and fun conversations
On the seventh day of Christmas my soul mate gave to me…
Companionship that only comes from a beautiful soul
On the eight day of Christmas my soul mate gave to me…
An ear of listening with compassion
On the ninth day of Christmas my soul mate gave to me…
The ability to trust her in absolute
On the tenth day of Christmas my soul mate gave me…
A belief set and Character that rival Virgin Mary
On the eleventh day of Christmas may soul mate have to me…
Submission with wisdom … even if I think she's better … I love her
humility
On the twelfth day of Christmas my soul mate gave to me…
A seed… many, many beautiful children!!!!
If you gave me those things… I couldn't ask for more my dear

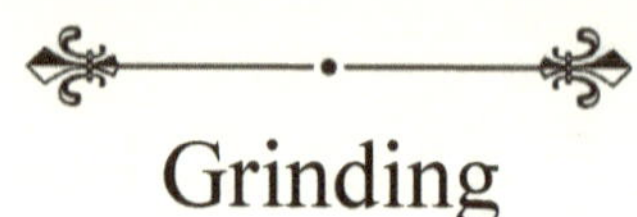

Grinding

Like a moth to the flame
I'm addicted to the grind

Like a fish in the sky
I'm outta place on this earth

Like stones under a waterfall
I feel the weight of a nation

like a starved lion
I'm hungry for the fight

Like a volcano ready to erupt
I hold the pain inside

Like a magician and His wonders
I amaze with the truth

Like storms across the sky
I bring misery to crooks

Like a rainbow after heavy rainfall
Hope is restored where once was none

Like fools to the wise
I'm an enigma to the faithless

Like the path of a bullet train
I don't stop till I reach my destination

Like horror to the harmless
I fear I may never make it home

Like controversy on a sunny day
My own thoughts betray me

Like a homerun to win the game
I'd lay my life down for victory

Like bees and their need for honey
I can't live without your love dear

Like extreme danger to the youth
My life hangs in the balance

Like depression to the hopeless
My emotions betray me

Like a grizzly outta hibernation
I'm getting ready to annihilate

Like I bird learning to fly
I'm on the path to rise above

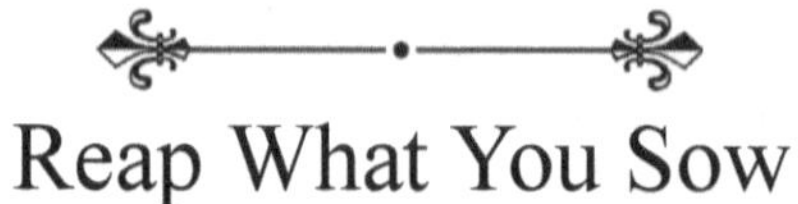

Reap What You Sow

Peace belongs to those
Who waged war for good

Resolve belongs to those
Who seek the greatest alternative

Family belongs to those
Who seek brotherhood

Glory belongs to those
Who fight for what's right

Strength belongs to those
Who fought the hardest

Wisdom belongs to those
Who diligently sought the truth

Courage belongs to those
Who won't back down

Enlightenment belongs to those
Who sought a higher understanding

Hope belongs to those
Who never gave up

Joy belongs to those
Who've seen the most pain

Life belongs to those
Who hate the slaying of innocent

Character belongs to those
Who wage war on personal evil

Devotion belongs to those
Who have the most zeal

Power belongs to those
Who treat the least and greatest with fairness

Mercy belongs to those
Who were merciful

Greatness belongs to those
Who can suffer the most

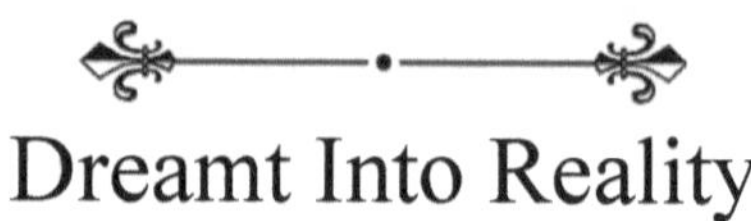

Dreamt Into Reality

I dreamt her into my life
Nothing

I prayed her into existence
Nothing

I wooed her hope she'd respond
Nothing

I tried and tried looking driving searching
Nothing

I mailed her a letter
Nothing

I poured my heart and soul out
Nothing

I must be a madman
Cause I still believe she's real
And I love her to pieces
LORD GOD PLEASE!!

Thus the Reward

Hardship when worn right becomes strength
Curiosity when placed in the right direction becomes discovery
Questions when sought correctly become wisdom
Imagination when used in the correct manner becomes invention
Losses when directed become tools for improvement
Mistakes when taken into account become understanding
Sorrow when understood becomes gratefulness
Responsibility and the weight of it all leads to contentment
Destruction and a helping hand show you mercy
Dreaming without fail leads to hope
Taking a shot despite your fears creates courage
Battling your demons shrinks their control over you leaving inner peace
Forgetting the pain leads to healing
Admitting you aren't perfect can lead to forgiveness
Spending time repenting begets character
Poison leads to a stronger tolerance
Redemption is only possible if you first fall away
Wasting time with the Divine begets Holiness

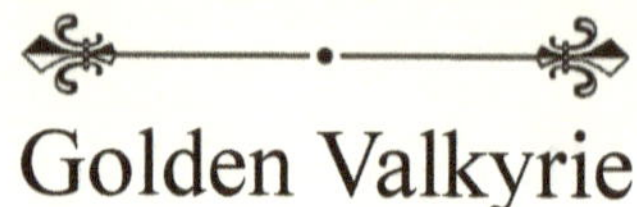

Golden Valkyrie

She shined forth as a Valkyrie of light
Using wisdom and truth as arrows
Piercing the fools who thought they were wise
Showing her colors of wisdom
She stood courageously
Unafraid of the bigheaded low-minded fools
Staying pure as a maiden of morality
She fought valiantly for the underprivileged
Rising as a beacon for her people

I Love You You Give me Meaning

My heart is a stone without your love
Hard cold and empty
Without void or understanding
As the earth before creation

My mouth is empty flow of gibberish
Without your ears to listen
What good is my words without you?
You're the one I want to bond with as one

My mind is brutish and incomprehensible
Without a partner to give it meaning
A mad man of incomprehensible insanity
But by you understanding you get me,
Taken me to new heights

My eros is nothing
I am asexual; purity at its finest without her
The prettiest girls look like just another human
But you, dear woman, you complete me
You make me a romantic where once was selfishness
Your turn on my desire like food to the obese
Freeing my unsexuality and creating a drive
Only for you, always
My one and only

Surreal Angel

I imagined her…
As an angel in thy skies
Coming down in perfection
Being the perfect soul to compliment mine
But she was better than all that

I dreamt of her
Her personality lively and exuberant
Her mind full of question and wonder
Her heart pure and honest as a child
But she surpassed my wildest imaginations

I worried about her
That she would do too much for me
That she would suffer to save me
That she loved me so much she would be in pain for me
But as much as I tried to protect and be there for her
She was the one that saved me

For without her
I am an empty tomb
A soulless body
And a lifeless corpse
But with her I shine
As the brightest of angels

A Whisper

A whisper
I heard it softly
So gently
So kindly
Saying
I love you
Don't be afraid

A voice
Speaking clearly
Distinctly
With care
Saying
I always protected you
And I always will

A cadence
So, crystal clear
So distinct
Such depth
Saying
I never left you
I've been by your side
Without fail I'm yours

Death by Torment

The masses congregated
Had me chained up
They all pointed the finger at me
With their guns
But one soul came forth
And took the shots

I cried terribly disgusted
How could I let someone take the fall?
I felt such disgrace
Such inward shame
I cried out telling her to run
But she didn't listen

I wanted to die that day
I had broken the minds of demons
I had spoken words knowing the consequence
So, I was ready to lay my life down
I wanted no one to die but me
But she took the fall
And I wept bitterly

As they tormented me worse than death
If hell is on earth, it's when a woman takes the fall for a man
Why do you want power?

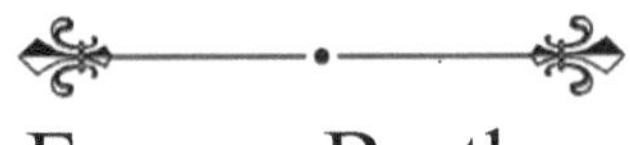

For my Brethen

I desired power
Not for myself
But to protect others
To defend the helpless
To level the playing field
And look out for the little man

I craved direction
Not for me
I wanted to know
The ways to lead and to guide
To show others how to make it through
And the best route for their souls

I asked for pain and sorrow
For me to take myself
To be a beacon of light
And hope the hopeless
So that those that suffer likewise
Can say "He's been there
And he's just like me
So maybe I can endure"

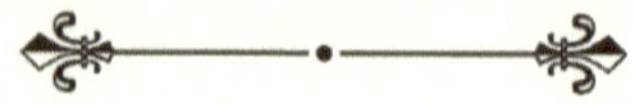

What We Bring to the Table

Woman this is what you bring to the table
Loyalty
Faithfulness
Comradery
Love
Humility
Passion
Goofiness
Excitement
An ear
Caring
Submission
Beauty
Sexiness
Stunningly good looks
A standout babe
The perfect set of eyes
Great major assets
Gorgeous blond hair
I know I said physicals matters least and it does but… everyone
notices looks sorry I still value her soul most important
What I bring to the table
My love
My words
My companionship
My beard
My blue eyes
My loyalty
My manliness
My heart
My soul
My obsession

We Haven't Even Met… But You've Given Me So Much Already

You gave me hope
That there was someone else
Someone like me
Who agreed with me
Who would bring me joy
And compliment me

You gave me goals
Something to seek for
A goal to become worthy of
Something to be Holy for
To give up the evil I'm me
And choose the light

You gave me excitement
That maybe there was someone
Who would get me
And follow my God
And chase my dreams with me
As we embrace each other
In perpetuity

# Love DNA

My DNA don't lie
My love for you…
Is part of my DNA
It cannot be altered
I was born with it
Taking it away would be
Stripping me of my being
My desire for you
Is deeply intertwined
With my soul
My soul wouldn't be
Without its desire for you
Because your apart of it
I wouldn't have a chance
to be one with anyone
If it weren't for you

Souls Belong

As crops need rain
Or the earth needs the sun
My soul is void without you
You bring me pain apart/joy together
Death comes to us all
But do you know what's more
Terrifying then death?
Me being without you
Because death comes quickly
But my regret for you would be eternal
Pain comes to us all
But do you know
What bring the most pain?
The idea that we can't be together
It's painful just waiting
But never meeting is torment
The highest expression in joy
Cannot be expressed in mere words
Because you bring that to me
Even apart imagining you and
Writing you my love gives me
More depth than the ocean

They Say Coal is Diamonds So It Is

The crazy one spoke
    But his words fell off the deep end
    And all saw his insanity
Society moved on

The harsh one spoke
Words of bondage
But all saw his yoke
Society moved on

The irrational spoke
Words impossible
But all saw its fallacy
Society moved on

The persuader spoke
Speaking diamonds of coal
Appealing to the deprived
But most saw his trick

The swindler swindled
Speaking of the rarity of coal
And the abundance of diamonds
Fooling only fools

The propagator persisted
Pushing them paradise to the children
Wearily some caved

Seeking that diamond of coal
The dissenter rebelled
But it was too late
Coal was diamond now

The sane were crazy
The gentle harsh
The rational irrational
As paradise became hell

.

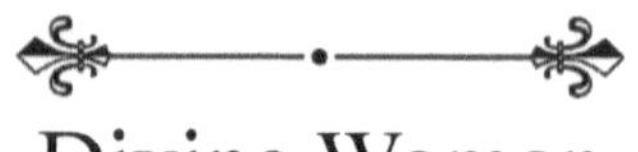

Divine Woman

I dreamt of her
Her honest pure mouth
With nothing to hide
Putting knaves to silence
Her personality shining
As bright as electricity
Warming those surrounding her
And fending off ruffians
Her emotions in tune with divine angles
As she cries over injustices
And rejoices in the humble
Who rises victorious
Her eyes show the depth
Of a soul driven through fire
Ready to tackle any obstacle
And give thanks for hardships
Her belief in God steady as a rock
Unquenchable love of her Savior
Praising thanking and walking with Him
Every day as she grows closer to the Divine

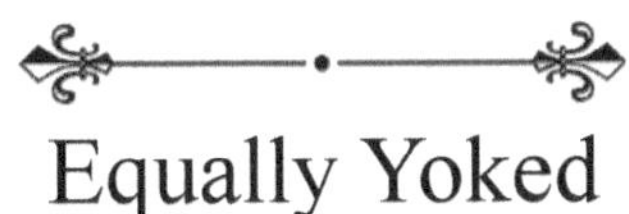

Equally Yoked

I waited for her eagerly
Counting the stars above
Praying to the God of Creation
Hoping that she exists
With nothing but a dream

God asked me why?
Why is she so important to you
Why do you need her
Why not anyone else?
Why do you love her?

I told God I didn't have much to me
So, I wanted someone that made life worthwhile
I'm lonely and don't belong anywhere
One wife and I might as well aim for the moon

I know she loves you like I do so it'll work
The nights got long alone
The days seemed meaningless
Without her to share them with

Like I was a shell of what I could be
And women all seemed this or that
But she was everything I sought
And she belongs with you as I do

Somebody Save Me

All I heard was doubt
All I knew was rejection
Why I held on hope is beyond me
I still feel like a reject
Like a throwaway rag
But I believed she was out there
Someone that accepted me
That forgave me
That chose me above all else
Like I did to her

And when we meet,
A piece of me will die
The dark hatred of self
As I finally see someone
That proves I have worth
Because she was made for me
And I for her

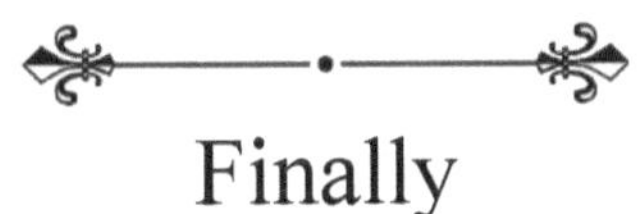

Finally

I've found her!!!
The girl of my prayers
The angel from God !!!
Goodbye ignorance
Hello intimacy!

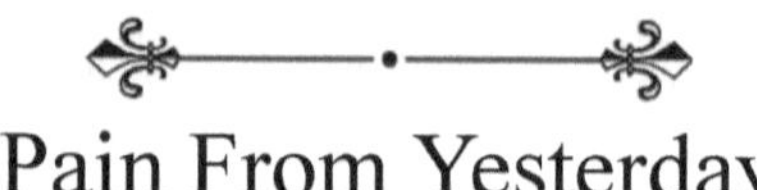

Pain From Yesterday

It made me lonely
In a room full of people
None could bring laughter to my heart
And everyone felt like a stranger
Even the closest of kin
It made me easy tasks monumental
Each simple action taking its toil
Draining the lifeblood from me
Wearing me to the core
Forcing me to give it my all just to get by

The emotions were gone
Just a lingering weight
Replacing the simple joys
And giving me heavy sorrows
Yet "This too shall pass"
My tears and prayers will be answered

I look back in my life
Seeing the pain constantly
Feeling it as if I were there
Wondering how I made it
Thanking God that time moves forward

I reminisce of yesteryear
The joy!! the wonders!!!
Overshadowed by grief and letdowns
Everywhere in my past
Thankful all things move forward

Yesteryear

I remember the past
So much to do with my life
So many options to take
But I fear I take the easy path
Wondering if I could have done more

I recollect my history
And become grateful for the past
I realize mistakes taught me
Weights strengthened me
And God always had my back

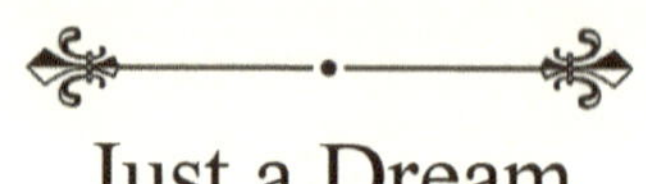

Just a Dream

I dreamt of her
With my waking eyes
All her righteous qualities
All her love and loyalty
Someone made for me

But it was just fantasy
My imagination went rampant
Dreaming of the impossible
My mind played tricks on me
Woman aren't dreamt up by man
With every fiber of my being

I wished she were real
I hoped it was more than a dream
I wanted to make dreams a reality
But that isn't within my power

I wanted someone to cherish and love
Who was worthy of my suffering
And pushed me to be more
Because she was everything
And I was everything to her
And Christ was everything to us, as one

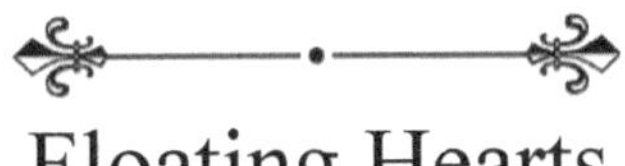

Floating Hearts

My soul drifts here and there
Seeking depth substance and truth
Asking the hard questions
That can't be answered audibly
Seeking solace and a resting place

My mind wonders in oscillation
Seeking wisdom humor or the right words
Hesitating outta fear of failure
Always giving it my all
Seeking to be the best it can be

My heart floats on steadfast
Seeking one to share its love with
Finding none worthy of it
Only those who abuse and use
Praying to the Creator of hearts
Seeking her the answer to my prayers

My Love Remains

Take away my emotions
Bury them deep within
A cold robot I'd become
Yet love is an action
And you bring out my best in me

My love for you would still remain
Waiting to see you, to break free
Take away my will
The urge to go on no more
A wandering soul drifting
With no path to follow

Yet deep down I'm holding on
My love for you would remain, keeping me
Pushing me forward to be with you
Take away my sanity

The logic of love lost
The muscle of mental health vanished
Giving me cloudy thoughts
And dark chaotic possibilities
Yet my love dear woman will remain
Keeping me loyal to the promises for her

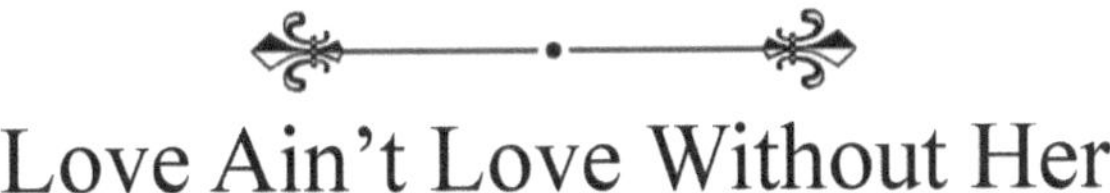

Love Ain't Love Without Her

I conquered my demons
Struggling with their throws
And continuous attacks
Finally at peace with myself
Yet I'm nothing without her

I accomplished wonders
Wrote words of beauty and elegance
Transpired poetry transcending veracity
Yet I long for her sweet love

I understood secrets
Hidden from the whole world
Truths that took me a trip to hell to discover
Yet all seemed wasteful without her presence
I sought after love

I found love here and there
From friend acquaintances and strangers
All there for me but I feel empty
That deep connection between man and woman
The kind that makes two one

That transcends logic
And makes love between the two
Cover every facet of the being
And combine them to one entity of completeness
She is perfect for every part of me

My Whole Being Yearns for Her

My mind
Searches for a voice of reason
A wise woman who seeks after truth
And despises knaves and wheedlers
Who understands right from wrong
And speaks the words of comfort

My body
Desires a soul that keeps herself pure
No ugly stains on her perfect skin
No metal hooks to contaminate
Only pure raw natural beauty
That has no nothing to hide

My soul
Wants the one and only
The matching mate that matches me
The passion that driving both of us together
Equal to mine in worth and talent
That shines like the sun in the darkest of night

My heart
Pleads for a heart of compassion
A beautiful merciful partner
That desire good even for her enemies
Who pleads for the less fortunate
And aids the down and out

My personality
Seeks the correlating star
Funny serious and deep
Carefree steadfast and believing
She who gets me and returns the favor
With words of comfort joy and laughter
If I exist she must

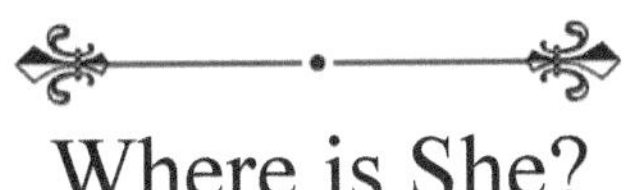

Where is She?

I failed
Miserably I sought after love
Seeking one worthy
Never finding one to call mine

I prayed
Diligent I sought a higher power
To solve this crisis within
Time after time I poured out my soul

I wrote to her
An imaginary figure
Hoping she was real
The one id be one with

I'm waiting
Calling out to her endlessly
Wooing her with my best
Knowing she must exist
Because I do

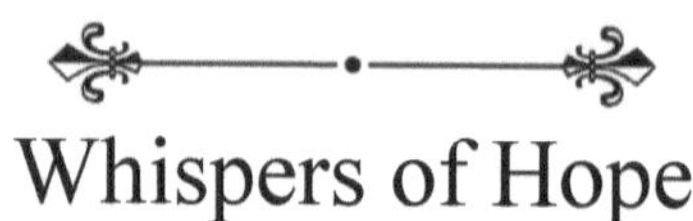

Whispers of Hope

The mountain looms overhead
Reaching to the heavens
Surrounding with no other options
Overwhelming our weary hearts
A whisper in our hearts:
"Every mountain shall be brought low"

Loss after loss I experience
Felt I've lost the best parts of me
Weeping so much no tears are left
Heart in the gutter from loss
Yet a whisper in my heart
"O death where is thy sting…"

I seek for joy everyday
Everything seems so empty
Nothing satisfies my empty soul
Everyone goes their own way
I cry out in desperation
A whisper lingers in my heart
" I am the Bread of Life"

I'm weighed down heavily
The tasks of life overwhelm
The sacrifices for my loved ones
Daily taking its toll on me
With nowhere to turn
But a voice whispers in my heart
"Come to me all ye heavy laden and I will give you rest"

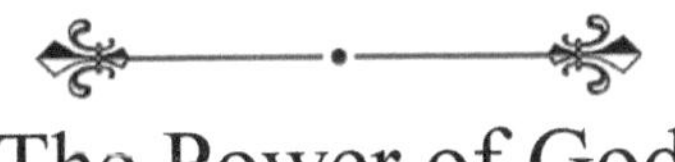

The Power of God

I believed in myself
After years of inner turmoil
It seemed to go well
I thought I could succeed
But I came to realize
I couldn't do it on my own

My vanity got me high
But when I went alone, I fell
Sinking like heavy metal
I realized I needed more
More than just self

I sought aid through others
I trusted them
They did the best they could
They gave me as much as I gave them
Together we accomplished some
But we fell short

I wanted so much more
But we just weren't enough
Failure after failure
Turmoil after turmoil
Proved even together
Just ain't enough

I had nowhere else to turn
Was life a joke?
A painful realization of failure
A haunting memory of shortcomings
Yet I sought the Living God
A faith in the Higher Power

Hoping to find meaning

His Word spoke to my heart
Saying that faith in Him
Was the only faith that lasted
That He couldn't fail
That even in our failures
There was a silver lining
Of a soul enriched by His power
My future lover

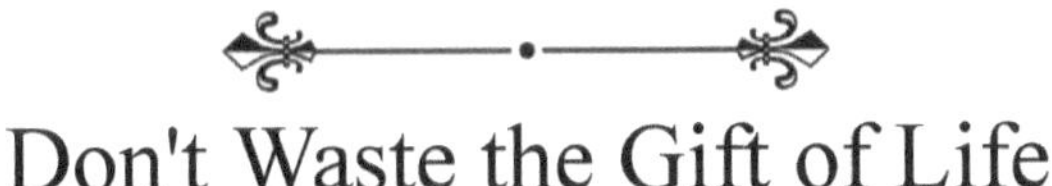

Don't Waste the Gift of Life

What good is a heart?
With no one to share it with?
With no one to love more than feelings
With no one to sacrifice for
With no one to call your lover

What good is a mind?
If it stays to itself
And shares nothing with another
Keeping all its secretes and talents
Locked up within

What good is a soul?
Alone wandering the earth
With no equal no better half
No one to calm it in the rough times
And illuminate it in the good

Look Deeper, Beyond the Flaws

I wanted the world
The moon and the stars
Best life with the best woman
A wonderful set of kids
But I had nothing to give
Nothing to earn it with
Or prove my worth deserved that

I wanted the best attributes
Strength of the heart
Courage to die for those I loved
Wisdom to know when to fight
But I was shallow and vain
With nothing to say
And little interactions to prove
My worth to obtain such gifts

I desired greatness for myself
To rise above my struggles
To be strong in the face of adversity
And conquer my demons perpetually.
To be there for others when I was in pain
But I was pathetic
Unwise cowardice weakness
Those were my strengths

I couldn't even save myself
What business did I have
Giving my hand of help out others
when both of us would sink?
I looked in the mirror
And saw the most frightening thing
Helpless alone confused

Searching for a way out

Everything boring me
While at the same time overwhelming
But I looked deeper within
Deeper beyond the blues that consumed
And I saw determination
I saw hope in a higher hope

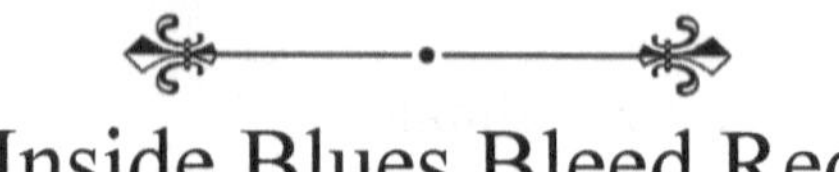

Inside Blues Bleed Red

Pain that could be healed
And the force within growing
Ready to forget forgive and conquer
I kept the pain inside so the world wouldn't worry
I looked inside my blues
And found bloody red pain
Surrounding me circling my body
Ready to escape the body
And spill my bloody pain everywhere

But I focused on the blue
Holding all that pain inside
Keeping the worst of me inside
While trying to shed rays of hope
Battling optimism and heaviness

Yet the red kept me going
The painful bloodiness within
Kept the strength inside
While showing the carefreeness
And bliss of my baby blues
That gave the whole world hope

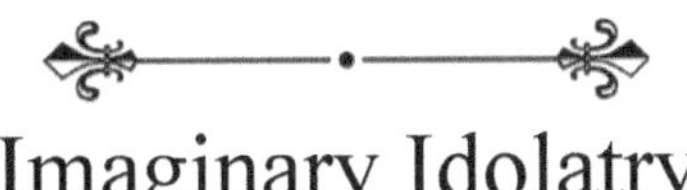

Imaginary Idolatry

I tried giving her up
But she was never there.
How can one give up what one doesn't have?
A dream perhaps… give up your dream
But this isn't a dream or a goal or a hope
It's concrete fact of feeling
How can I stop loving if it doesn't exist?
Unless it does but it's just not tangible…
Air cells faith all exist without being seen
So, my love… she must be real
For how can I feel this passionate
About a fake person?
How can we be together apart?
When we've never seen talked or even greeted
How can two love without their other half?
One day… one day soon
We will complete our broken halves
We will prove that eros exists….

Strange Questions

The best answers
Often come from the strangest questions
How does one know an answer
Unless first a question is conceived?

To wander the mind is to dare to ask
Creativity begins with curiosity
But solidifies itself with truth

Ask is the first step to receiving
Seeking the first step to finding
And wondering the first step to discovery

Desire without limits leads to obsession
Obsessions leads to cloudy mind
And clouded mind to mistakes

Can desire be satisfied?
For how long to what limit
Or does it burn uncontrollable like the sun,

Never achieving its goal
Is desire the opposite of satisfaction?
What is meaning without understanding
Or virtue without truth?

If love is an action how do perform it?
How do I let her know
I
Love
Her

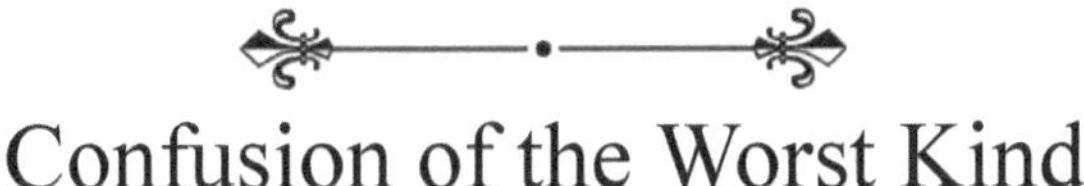

Confusion of the Worst Kind

The worst type of confusion
Is the kind you aren't confused about
Where you are so certain
That you'd lose your mind

When lies and "truth" are swapped
When you've been taught lies all your life
That two plus two equal 5
That science cannot falter
That history only has one side

When your world is flipped
Can you withstand the propaganda
When science lies for money
When history is altered for power
When math manipulated
Will you be able to go on
Knowing the good guys aren't
And everyone has an agenda

Would you rather stay ignorant
As the world burns to chaos
Than wake up to a war
For the soul of mankind?

Mercy Trumps Righteousness

Being right
Isn't as important
As being merciful

Being wrong
Isn't as bad
As being conceited

Being the last
Doesn't mean as much
As finishing

Being alone
Means little
If you've got a good foundation

Losing yourself
Is only a concern
If you never come to your senses

Talking a big game
Is all rhetoric
Unless you are willing to put in the hours

Running away
Can always be solved
By returning to where you belong

Being afraid
Is just a process
Of overcoming your fears

Seeking love

Takes trial and error
But if you get it right endures

Living a life worthy of praise
Requires sacrifice dedication and diligence
For all will be revealed in time

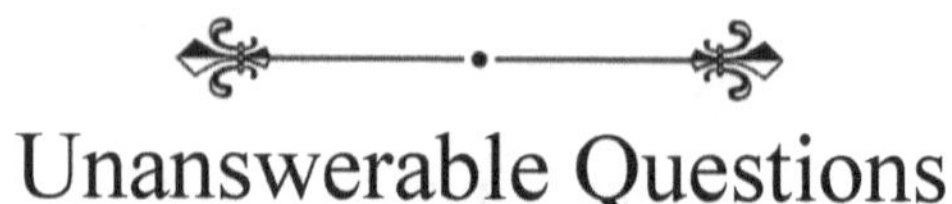

Unanswerable Questions

When you falter
Where do you run?

When you make a mistake
Who do you blame?

When you fail
Who do you go to?

When the world seems big
What shrinks it for you?

When you're all alone
Who do you think of?

When you're your own worst enemy
Who is your greatest ally?

When you can't find a way out
Who do you turn to?

When right is wrong and up is down
Who is your council?

When fear is greater than sanity
How do you see clearly?

When you fall more than rise
Whose there to pick you up?

If the greatest ally betrays
Where would you turn?

The Law of Love

Love is free as air
   Yet costly as life
   Love is as wild as the ocean
And as tame as the sky
Love is as infinite as the cosmos
Yet as intimate as a cell
Love is as savage as the wilderness
And as clean as water
Love is immensely rewarding
Yet requires immense labor
Love is as humbling as failure
Yet empowering as success
Love is tears over loss
Yet laughter over gain
Love is gratitude over company
And despair over separation
Love is faith for the best of times
And hope in the worst of times
Love is logic for confusion
And confusion when you lose it
Love is peace of mind in action
And giving of thanks to others
Love is ruling over with compassion
And serving with dutiful obedience

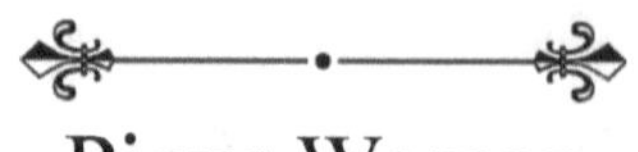

Pious Woman

I saw her
Reading the scripture
Singing the hymns
Walking with God
But it was just a dream

I heard her
Helping the less fortunate
Sacrificing for her family
Being there for her friends
But it was just a voice from my dreams

I witnessed her
Taking up her cross
Rejection the way of the world
Giving up her idols and lusts
But it was my imaginary daydreaming

I chose her
The loyal partner
The perfect match
The best friend
But she wasn't real!!!
It was just my burning desire

Love of the Unknown Lover

Love of the unknown lover
She was never there
But I wanted her to be
I dreamt of her beauty
I wrote her poems
I prayed earnestly for her
I wanted to will her into existence

Unsuccessfully
I had nothing to go by
Just pure willpower
A hope that I had a better half
Voices in my head telling me
She was everything I wanted and more

But I knew nothing about her
In reality it was imaginary vanity
I dreamt of her inward beauty
I desired a personality perfect for me
I wished for a perfect companion
That would make me forget all others

Vainly adding more and more expectation
Receiving nothing to consolidate my heart
Fruitlessly seeking her: the nonexistent
Amidst all this confusion
I couldn't give her up
I desired her so fiercely
I don't want just a lover or just a wife
I wanted someone more
Something to complete me
Who would reciprocate the love I gave
And make my barren soul whole

If I Could Have Any Woman

If I could choose any woman in the world
Id search for you alone
I'd see the most praised
The most glorified for their beauty
The highest decorated for their body
And say "I'd rather be with my beauty"
Because in my eyes she's more beautiful

If women had everything to offer me
The most money to give me a life of luxury
The most esteemed positions they could offer me
The funniest best personality to be with me
The most faith to move mountains
I'd say I'd rather be with my women
Because in my eyes she has more to offer

If women were to be the best at anything
The best lover to make me in heaven
The most loyal that would always be there for me
The most divine with angel like qualities
The best friend that would complete me
I'd say your either a bold face liar
Or you haven't seen my woman
Cause she's all that to me

For Eva (Sorry Soul Mate)

Those eyes
Those beautiful baby blues
The centerpiece of her beauty
Showing that compassionate soul
Forefront for that brilliant mind
Bursting into life
Shining forth as the sapphire sky

Gorgeous hair flowing wild and free
An amazing body that most women envy
And men can't take their eyes off
Class in every way she glows with grace
But it's the eyes that shine most brilliant
The gateway to the soul
And are the epitome of beauty

For what good is a body
Without the ability to see
And what good is looking
If there's no color to brighten the mood
And what color is more perfect
To express the calm soothing peace
Than that divine shade of heavenly blue

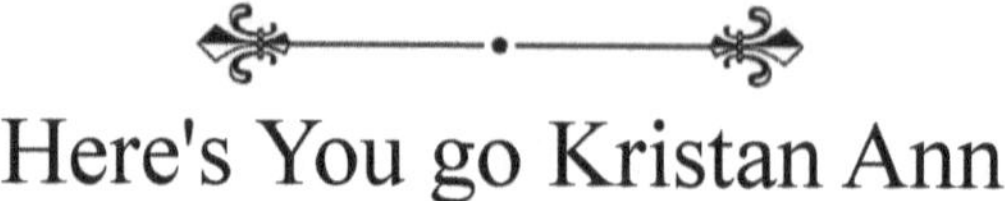

Here's You go Kristan Ann

She wants to shine forth with the best of them
Show off her beauty and prowess
But they reject her
They say she can easily be replaced
But I see no one worthy of her legacy

They mock her for her chastity
For her loyalty to God
And her saving herself for the right man
But I've never seen such beauty
Such glorious dedication to the truth

She dedicates her life to a higher power
Spreading love and cheer
To as many as she meets
Fighting for the weak and helpless
Her beauty transcends the physical realm

Lost Cause

I lost hope
The bad guys won
They said racisms bad
It's bad to judge others
Your people are worse
You are privileged
You have it so good

Others suffer because of you
They came as good people
We just want equality
So long as your people are on the bottom
And everyone else benefits
You don't know how hard it is to be them
You should pay them back for what you did to them
As they stole our land jobs women and country

They fooled our women
The most gullible of all
The easiest way to attack
"Men are evil... be independent"
"Do whatever you want don't be a slave to men"

Feminism just doing whatever you choose there's nothing wrong with that
Date minorities... they love you better... they deeper… will be more exciting
Don't be mother's- that beneath you-unless it's with a minority
Be a rebel- murder your baby- destroy the beauty of your natural body
They raise our kids as our parents were taxed
They showed them sex in elementary school
They pushed sexuality on them
Even forced some to mutilate themselves

Told others they were gay or lesbians and that was good
Pushed drag queen and pedophilia as a good thing
Told our kids white people are the problem
Told them they're evil and the root cause of oppression

Jews controlled everything
The porn the banks the media the entertainment the government
Asians and Indians got great jobs
Blacks killed raped and murdered like vermin while we could not speak a word against
Hispanics were the highest percentage of pedophiles as they stole our land illegally
Muslims couldn't be touched for their crimes while they hated America
Yet whites are the problem in a nation created and built by white men

And we white men couldn't criticize anyone or we were evil for being bigoted racist homophobic xenophobic
Our white men took the burden of a falling nation
They were last in line for any privilege
Least likely to get a job cause everything was against them
Least likely to get into schools cause they were white men and everything was easy for them
Nearly impossible to find a decent woman

Was forgotten in politics and every major field despite their brilliance
They were blamed for their masculinity as if that's a problem
Rejection scorned broken and mocked they still held firm
And one day they will raise up and turn this lost cause into freedom justice and truth
I'm lonely… are there any pro-life anti LGBTQF anti feminist pro white girls that wanna have a good conversation?????????

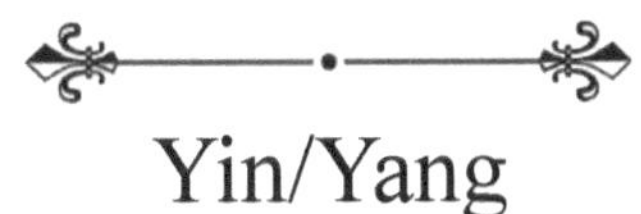

Yin/Yang

Without loss
I would never know victory
Without pain
I could never find healing
Without hate
I wouldn't understand love
Without despair
I would never grasp hope
Without danger
Safety wouldn't be important
Without fear
Peace of mind wouldn't be
Without distractions
Focus wouldn't be needed
Without evil
What is good?
Without sacrifice
How would we show we care?
Without strangers
How could we have brotherhood?
Without death
How could there be life?
Without time
How could forever exist?
Without woman
How could there be man?
Without you
How could there be us?

Put Yourself Out There

Those who never question
Blindly follow their masters
Don't explore beyond
And never find what their soul thirsts for

Those who never dare
Look normal like the rest
Fit in a typical lifestyle
But never untap their potential

Those who never love
Are an empty shell of a soul
Seeking selfish desire
And die alone without comfort

Those who never wonder
Live in an enclosed world
And blankly glance at the stars
With body vacant of the soul

Those who never dream
Live for the present timeframe
Chasing nothing but instant satisfaction
Living like a man without freedom

Would You... Keep Your Promise

I waited a thousand years
Would you still love me?
Or would you need others to sustain you?

If I promised you
Would you believe?
Would it be strong enough to keep you going?

If I faltered
Could you forgive?
How much could you take from me until you couldn't?

If I lost my mind
would you be there to heal?
how much could you take from my insanity?

If God asked me to die for Him
Would you be able to carry on?
Would you take care of our posterity and carry on?

If in heaven we weren't married
Would you still be my friend?
Would you still be into me after ten thousand years?

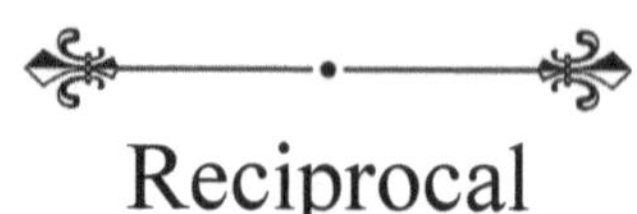

Reciprocal

If I exist… she must
If I feel pain… she must feel more
If I burn with passion… hers must be crippling
If I have a standard… her beliefs must align
If I miss her more than life… she must have waited ages
If I believe in truth… she must have a strong foundation
If girls desire me… boys must surround her relentlessly
If I have longing… she must feel like hell
If I have love for her… she must have uncanny love
If I want no other… she must have eyes just for me
If I believe in God… she must be a saint
If I have understanding… she must have a brilliant mind
If life is pain… she must be the silver lining
If diamonds are precious… she must be the perfect rock
If humans have worth… she proves it
If man was made for love…. woman was made to experience that
If twain become one… I want us to be one forever
If death separates us... we will reunite
If loneliness were a disease… she would be my cure
If sacrifice were the only way… I'd sell my world for her
If she loves me… I'll never let her go

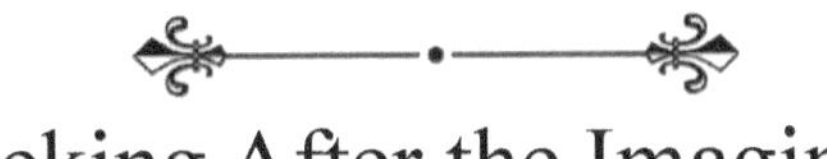

Seeking After the Imaginary

I sought her
An imagination?
A faulty dream?
A vain desire?
A selfish ambition?
Yet she seemed so real'

I thought of her beauty
Everywhere everyway all-consuming
Intertwined with her DNA
Not an ugly cell within
Only pure beauty
Emanating from her soul

I waited for her
Wasting time working
Wasting time eating
Wasting time sleeping
Wasting time waiting
Yet all this is worth it
Just to be with her forever

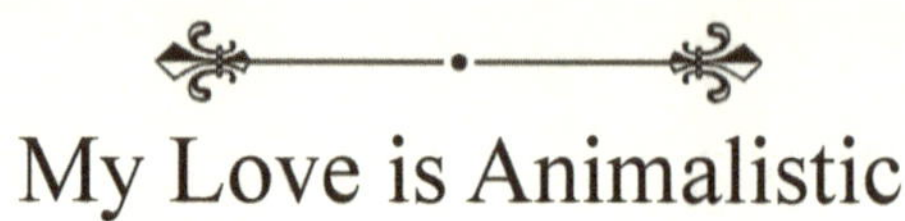

My Love is Animalistic

I long for you
As an airborne fish longs for water

I need you
As wolfs need a pack to belong

I feel alone without you
Like a bird of a feather with no together

I thirst for your presence
As a gazelle thirst for water in a Savannah

I hunger for your company
Like a staved bear in a roman coliseum

I desire suicide without you
Like a dolphin with no other of his kind

I think of you constantly
Like a bumblebee seeking honey

I lay traps to catch your heart
As a spider lays a web

I listen to your voice I'm my head obediently
As a perfectly trained water seals

I feel depressed Without you around
Waiting as a dog awaits his master

I travel over land and sea to migrant to you
As the migration of birds

I fight other males for your love
As a male lion wins over his mate

I stay loyal my whole life for you
As a penguin chooses the one and only mate for life

I Falter

I tried everything
But nothing seemed to work
In my mind
My assured delusional mind
She loved me
But I always loved her more

But how do you prove your love
To an unknown person
A nonexistent name
A fictional lover

But I still gave her everything
If I knew her
I'd do so much to make her happy
Because what is love but desiring the best for another?

Inner Peace For her

I want her to be comforted in times of sorrow
To be alleviated with words of cheer in time if pain
To be surrounded by a friendly face when she feels alone
To be held closely when she feels she's drifting away
To be taken care of when she feels overwhelmed
To be greatly desired when she feels unwanted
To be cherished with flowers so she can see beauty as I see hers
To be overwhelmed with love poems to let her know she has value
To be attended to so she knows that someone cares for her more than herself
To show her the world so she doesn't have to go alone
To hold her closely and wipe every tear away
Because her tears are precious diamonds to me
As it displays her beauty of compassion
And her weakness shows a beautiful soul
Willing to feel for lesser and display what's hidden beneath: care and concern: that you do give a care But I love your willingness to fight for what's right
I love your fortitude to stand strong on truth
And the fact you don't give up on people
And your loyalty… your glorious emerald of staying true even when you cut them off you still care
I
Loved
You
I'll love you more
You're gonna prove that you can be extremely beautiful inside and out
I won't give up on you
If you stay true to me, I'll fight valiantly
If love is eternal, we shall never separate

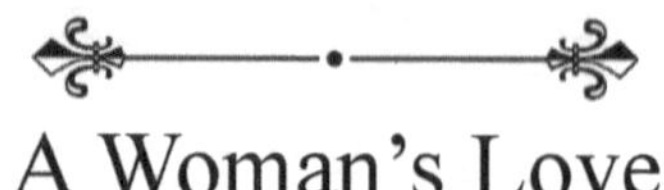

A Woman's Love

To love a woman
What the heck's the point
What do you get outta it
Why does it matter what they think

What is love but vanity
What is woman but confusion
They come for you deceptively
They make you play a silly game
They don't care if you wait forever
Just so long as they're taken care of

It's all about them
You cry out to them
Try to be honest
Try to be worthwhile
Try to develop something deeper

But they watch you suffer
As they pick another
Choosing you like sweaters
You pour out your heart and soul
Hoping for just one
That's all you want
Just one

But she makes you wait
She doesn't care about you
You're just there to make her happy
To say what she wants you to say
All for her

When The Voices Condemn God

I try to stand by Him
Because I want Him to be real
I want Him to be right
His ways are so perfect
His ways are without blemish
It all makes sense

He made the world
He made creation
But the voices condemned me
Promised me something better
But in my mind what can be better than a perfect loving just forgiving
God?

But the voices condemned me
I couldn't feel His presence
I couldn't hear His voice
I had lost the will to go on
Because He was the reason for Life

I became obsessed with an imaginary woman
I thought she could make me happy
I thought I could find something about myself
I just wanted to be friends with my God again
It seemed like He was punishing me
So, I couldn't speak to Him
Or Hear Him

I was so low
I replaced that love for God with her
That wretched soul I am!
That evil man of demons
And the voices condemned me for wanting God

They took my emotions of made me wanna support evil
But I just wanted her- and they used that against me
Where is my God????

MY GOD MY GOD WHY HAVE YOU FORSAKEN ME???
Please bring me back
I have no soul mate
I have no woman that can befriend me like you
There is no woman that mean as much as you do
And if the voices condemn me for this poem
I'm was nothing before I was created
And I'm still nothing apart from You

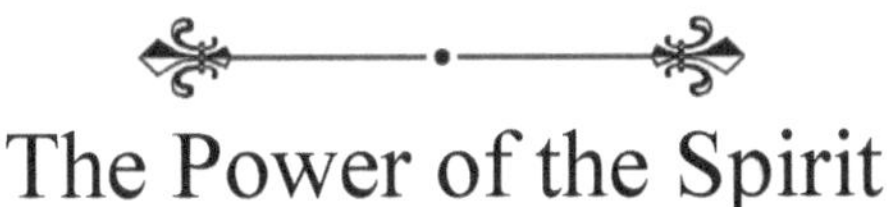

The Power of the Spirit

I was lost
With nowhere to turn
Nowhere to run and hide
Desperate for aid
I sought help anywhere
People couldn't cure the sorrow within
Others couldn't understand my troubles
They gave me no reason to live
But if I relied on His grace

It all made sense
And the pain eradicated
My spirit was weakened
By constant wear and tear
Everyday life worn it to the brim
The struggles within caused pain
It amplified the strife within
My spirit was in perpetual turmoil
But His spirit was enough
Not the strength the power or the might
But the Spirit itself gave life
Leaving me at ease with divine peace

Courage Wisdom Faith

I sought to be brave
I opened up my heart
I was scared to reveal my demons
But what Is courage really?
Is it standing up to the man?
Or fighting off your demons?
Courage from villains is carnage
Tackling you demons is the epitome of bravery

I desired wisdom
But I asked foolish questions
Again and again, I asked
To no avail but mockery
Until I realized though it all
By asking the foolish questions
The foolishness left me
Replaced by understanding

I doubted everything
My beginning my future
I didn't think I could last
I wasn't strong enough to do it
Not on my own
But a higher power
An omnipotent being
If I believed in Him
By seeking obeying and believing
I would do wonders

My Future Wife

I dreamt of her
Religiously following the good Word
Practicing the acts of truth and mercy
Living by faith without fear
Helping those around her like an angel
Without the recognition of a saint

I prayed for her
That she would stay true
To her convictions and beliefs
Tho the world tempts her right and left
That she stays loyal to her first love
As her love for others sees fruit

I desired her
To love cherish and hold her
As my one and only
To help her on her quest for justice
To aid her in her spreading of mercy
To seek the Higher Power together

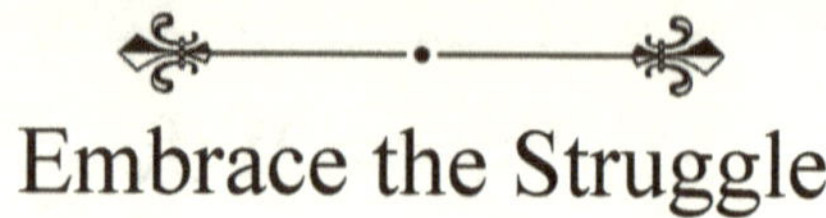

Embrace the Struggle

I sought strength
I fought a good fight
I bleed bruised and was beaten to a pulp
I went the distance only to lose

Why do I keep fighting?
All I do is fall short...
The pain seemingly overwhelming
how could I endure?

Feeling devastated by my failures
But I learned through it all
There can be no strength without pain
And came to embrace the struggle

What Would You Give for the Right Girl

When I met her face to face
The dream of my life
The hope of my prayers
The answer to the question
Am I alone in this world?

What would you give
To have a soul mate
To have an equal in worth
To look at a stimulating counterpart
To meet the girl of your dreams
What would you give?

What would you sell
To be closer to your better half
To communicate with more effectiveness
To understand their pains and struggles
And come together closer as one
What would you sell?

What would you sacrifice
To make your unity eternal
To stay together forever
With bonds of steel and love
Transcending space and matter
What would you sacrifice?

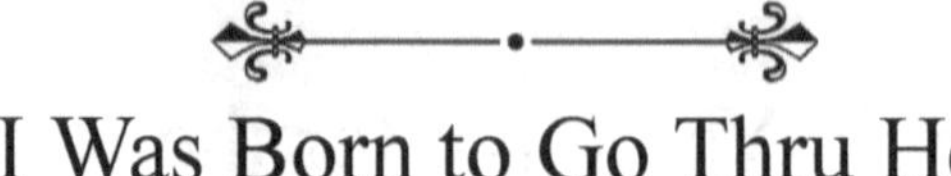

I Was Born to Go Thru Hell

I was born to go through hell
Battle my demons and rise above
Daily seeking forgiveness from God
While daily pushing myself to righteousness via faith

Finding my path upwards
I was born to sacrifice
To forgo my dreams aspirations and hopes
All for the pruning and testing of worth
Challenging myself hourly to self-control

To make myself an agent of goodness
I was born to love
To cherish the souls around me
And pray for all who cross my path
Hoping none suffer eternally
Even the worst of all I pray for mercy

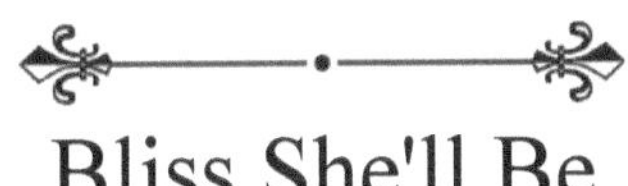

Bliss She'll Be

We wait in ecstasy
Just the thought of her
Made my heart pound jittery
As excitement floods my mind
With dreams of yesteryear flashing
Could this finally be the year?

After years of day dreaming
And tears from praying
All I have left is joy from hope
Of that soul that matches mine

All those years of doubting
Will be laid to rest
With one simple hello
I'll go from hell to heaven

As she makes me forget
The loneliness and sorrow
No more looking at girls
And wondering what ifs
I'm set for life with her
As my high goes to higher

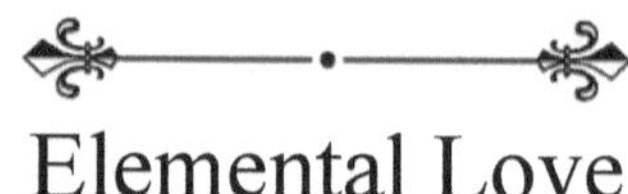

Elemental Love

As the sun shines by day
And gives its light to the moon by night
So, my love will never cease, by day or by night

As water fills the oceans
And covers the earth in rain
So too will my love cover you and reach you anywhere

As fire consumes forests
And spreads continuously
So too will my love consume you and continue evermore

As wind blows to and for
Surrounding us from every direction
So, my love will surround you wherever you go

As the earth gives you ground to walk on
And a place to rest your weary body
So too will my love serve you, giving you rest

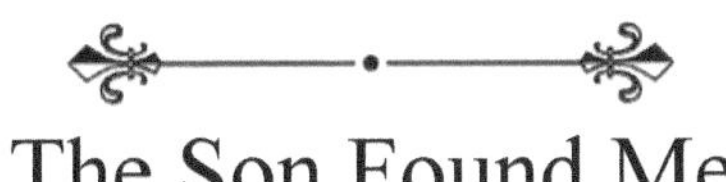

The Son Found Me

I searched for a way out
But got more lost
Until the Son found me

I sought after friends
but only found shallow fools
until the Son befriended me

I screamed from the pain
Helpless to find healing
Until the Son restored me

I felt empty and shallow
With no meaning or purpose
Until the Son gave me command to live

I felt wretched and devious
Disobeying all natural laws
Until the Son regenerated me

I felt abandoned and betrayed
With no one to go to
Until the Son rescued me

I felt in the valley of the shadow of death
Destined to burn for all eternity
Until the Son saved me from myself

I felt distant and far from God
Screaming profanities against His name
Until the Son brought light to my heart

I felt abused and molested

With no way out
Until the Son whispered to my heart

"I am the God of sorrow
Taking your pain on myself
That you may have joy forever"

Life With Me...

You'll see my demons
But understand my sainthood
It will be challenging
But will reap rewards
There will be hardships
But tremendous victories

There will be heavy sorrow
But tremendous joy
There will be rejection
But I will always be near
The hate will be uncanny
But the love ethereal

The struggles immense
But the good times aplenty
There will be echoes of silence
But smiles from the memories
It will require sacrifice
But bring tremendous gain

Life with me...
Will be a journey leading through hell
But winding up in heaven

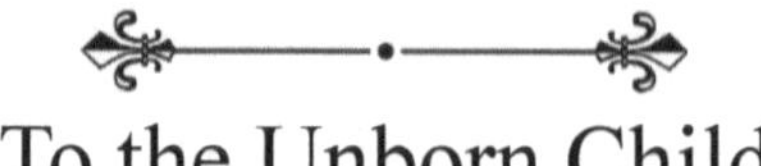

To the Unborn Child

To the unborn child....
  You will learn more than I know
  Seeing marvels
Watching discoveries
And making 90 the new 80

To the unborn child...
You will find love
Experience betrayal
And learn the art of conversation
And enjoy life to the fullest

To the unborn child...
You make a difference...
You are part something bigger
One man can make a difference
And I believe in redemption

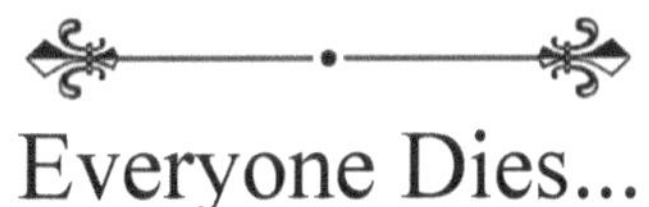

Everyone Dies...

What does it mean to live?
To really live??
We all die
But do we all experience life to the fullest?
Is it our relationships with others?
Maybe having a lot of friends?
Or having a deep personal friend?
Or raising a family?
Is it seeking truth?
Separating fact from fiction?
Seeking for the honest happenings?
Or searching for new light?
Maybe the answer lies in morality
Living by doing what's right?
By abiding by the highest standard?
And being dedicated to a life of value?
Or maybe Christianity is right?
Have a relationship with Christ... the best friend
Seek after the truth of the Bible … the way to heaven
Live after the morality of faith... the way of submission to righteousness
If there is a Creator… His way is life…for He created life

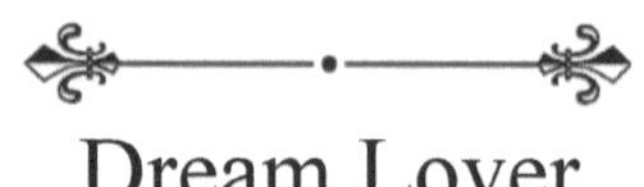

Dream Lover

I saw her
I hear her
I know her
But not personally
And it was eternal flames

I cried for her
I wept for her
I carried her burdens
But I couldn't wipe her tears
And it tormented me

I loved her
I cherished her
I gifted her with the gift of time
But I never got the chance to say I love you through the storm
And the storm broke me

I kept my promises
Never looked at another
Never wasted my breath with a lesser
But I may never meet her
My one and only joy

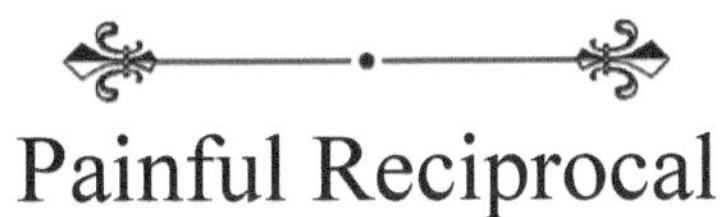

Painful Reciprocal

I cry for you
And you ignore
I weep
You smile
Why can't you see I'm yours?

I seek you
And you go about
I implore
You talk elsewhere
Why can't you understand me?

I write poetry
To persuade you
I write my life out
So, you get me
If you knew my level of love
You'd repeat it

You- You Complete Me

If I could find my better half
She'd complete it
Full of life and purpose

If I could understand logic
I'd seek her guidance
Because she is a rare woman of logic

If I could see beauty
I'd stare into her eyes
And gaze at serene depths of soul
That connects me to heaven

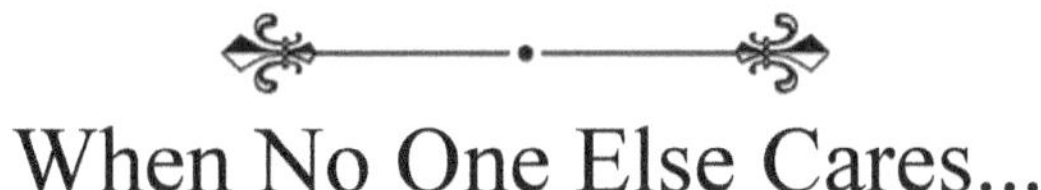

When No One Else Cares...

I remembered my home
But it was destroyed
I remembered my friends
But they abandoned me
I remember God
And we cried together

I sought peace
And it tore me to shreds
I sought virtue
And it taught me vice
I sought God
And we reasoned that life is hard

I sought her
But she didn't seek me
I sought elsewhere
But I didn't care
God said leave her
But I couldn't

I asked God why?
Why did I love her?
He said He wanted me to
That I'd be happier
But what if she doesn't love me?
I asked in tears
He said I love you more anyway

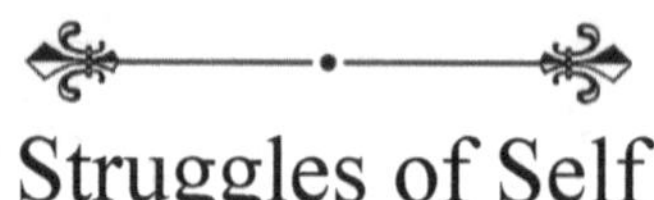

Struggles of Self

And I cried to myself like a baby
Saying
Why do I have no friends?
As I talked to myself without end

And I talked to myself without end
Thinking
Why am I so strange?
As I tried to solve everyone's problems but mine

And I solved no one's problems but my own
Struggling
Why?
Cause I give a care

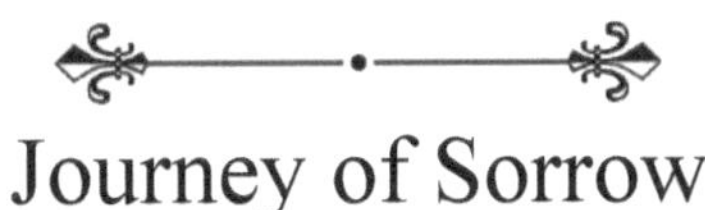

Journey of Sorrow

My friends abandoned me
I cried
Seeking one I found the lost boys
We cried together

I left my home
Lost and alone
No boys to help
I found sorrow

I sought a new home
I found her
We stop crying
As I said I love you

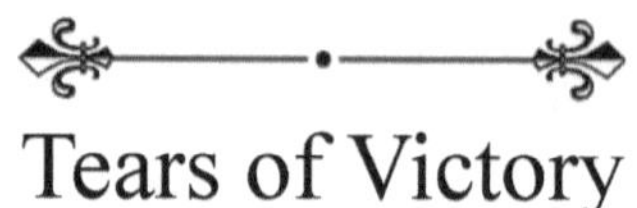

Tears of Victory

I wanted to die
But God said not today
I asked why
He said He had a plan
I laughed

Your plans, I said,
Always start in tragedy
But they end in joy He said
I looked up and smiled

It's always the same
I told Him hesitantly
I suffer get better and suffer
I laughed
He said
"One day there'll never be suffering...
Do you believe me?"
I cried

The Dark Side of Man

I sought peace within
But found strife
Wresting with my sanity
I couldn't tell if I was demon or beast

My inner self fought intensely
Was I an animal?
Could I call myself man?
What separates man, beast, and demon?

I cried to the Divine
He alone could give me a heart of flesh
I opened my eyes to see
And I looked at myself and saw no demon
And I gazed as the beast was made man

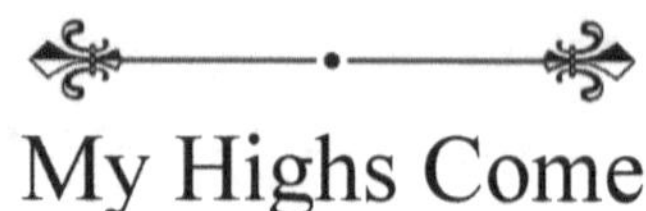

My Highs Come

When I think of our highs together
Just your thought brings ecstasy
My heart comes alive
When I fantasize of us together
Sharing moments of laughter and unity
My love feels volcanic

When I think of me becoming we
Replacing my wanting heart with bliss
My life seems worthwhile
When you make your entrance
Making elan outta mundane
My dreams become reality

When you show yourself
Surpassing my wildest dreams
My ramblings make sense
Cause someone finally gets me;)
As you respond with tact

My body's been kept pure
A holy temple waiting for you
As one becomes twain
My tomb is set in stone
You're the only one worthy to share it
Rising to the sound of our Savior
Together

My Love Will Remain Loyal

You were born to live with me
but one day you'll pass away and separate
Yet my love will remain loyal

You will laugh over joys
And you will cry from earthly pains
But my shoulder will always be open in love

You will ponder life
You will marvel at nature
While I stand by in harmony

You will discourse with philosophers
You will question scientists
Yet I will take you farther

You will experience inspiring wonders
You will experience heartbreaking sorrows
As my heart steadies us forward

You will find joy unspeakable
You will get lost in a world of awe
As I guide you home to the angels

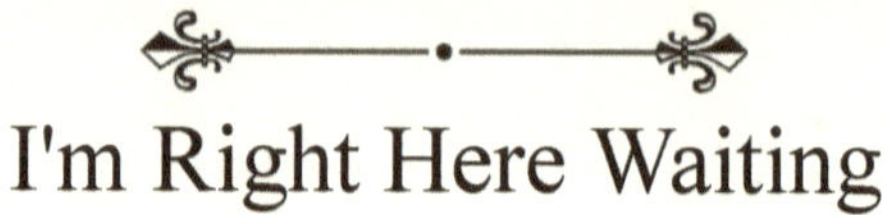

I'm Right Here Waiting

You seek comfort
You gaze for strength
I'm right here waiting
Strong as a rock, soft as a pillow

You seek for meaning
You desire purpose
I'm right here, waiting
Deep as the ocean wise as the sky

You've longed for love
You want more than words
I'm right here waiting
With a heart of flesh and words of stone

You speak riddles
You question life
I'm right here waiting
Rhyming your riddles and fulfilling your questions

You were born for more
You don't want to wind up alone
I'm right here waiting
Full of love and compassion

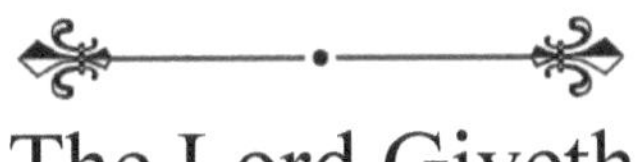

The Lord Giveth

God gave us mountains to conquer
God gave us valleys for reprieve
God gave us waters to purify
God gave us clouds to dream
God gave us trees to build
God gave us caves to explore
God gave us electricity to marvel
God gave us rain to wash away
God gave us air to breathe life
God gave us stars to shine on us
God gave us hills to rise above
God gave us beaches to relax with
God gave us animals to rule over
God gave us life to walk with Him
God gave us death to seek Him
God gave us His Son to know Him

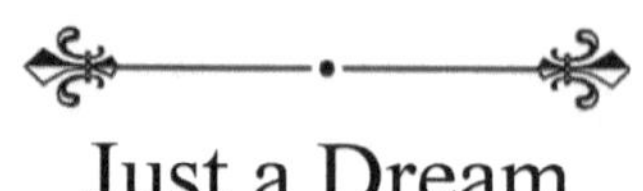

Just a Dream

I woke
Alone
She was just a dream
I gave up
Searching was useless
She wasn't near

I sent out
My calling card
praying
If we ever meet
It'll all be worth it
Loneliness will be no more

Eternal Crush

I hope our romance
Never ends
That we get that first crush feeling
And it never goes away
That I can't stop thinking of you
That I can't stop dreaming of you
That you stay my favorite person to talk to
That we never get old with each other
I hope when we get married
That honeymoon high
Never wavers or falters
But stays until our last breath
Never wavering

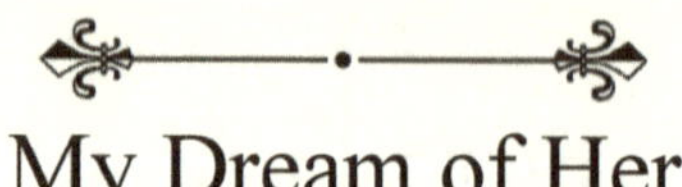

My Dream of Her

Some people have dreams
Of wealth
Of fame
Of power
My dream is her
Her time
Her love
Her hand forever
And my dream
Is to make her dreams
A reality
In this life and the next

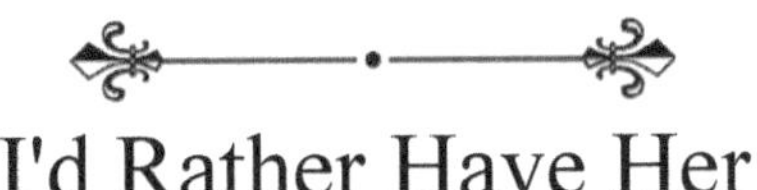

I'd Rather Have Her

If I had all power in the world
If I had all understanding
Or the gifts to excel at everything
I'd give it all for her hand

If I knew everyone
All the good
And became their friends
I'd leave them all for her

If I had to choose
Between a life of prosperity without her
Or a life of trial and hardship with her
I go through fire and scar myself
Just to wake up with her head next to mine everyday

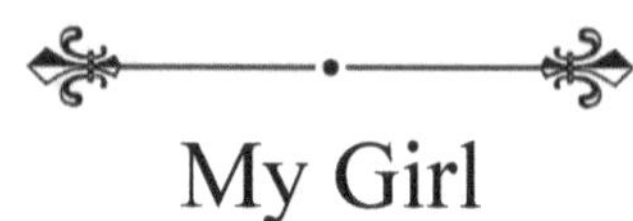

My Girl

What do I like about her?
Where does one begin??
She's more faithful than a dog
More kind than your grandma
More pure than all the angels
More innocent than a child
More just than a judge
More sweet than a cookie
More deep than the ocean
More virtuous than a saint
More character than a book
More interesting than a story
More intelligent than A.I
More dependable than a truck
More beautiful than a goddess
More hard working than a plumber
More logical than a puzzle
More fantastic than fantasy
More helpful than a recipe
More friendly than a pet
More patient than a sage
More wise than an owl
More forthright than a knight
More honor than a samurai
More loving than a mom
More compassionate than a doctor
More surreal than dreams
More humble than a child
More spirited than an actor
More amazing than Spiderman;) (MJ you are more amazing than me in
my mind)

Completion

How can man be without a helpmate?
How can one love without a woman?
How can one rest without weariness?
How can one help without knowledge?
How can one marvel without wonder?
How can one comfort without sorrow?
How can one solve without questioning?
How can one invent without curiosity?
How can one cry without emotion?
How one creates without creativity?
How can one bond without time?
How can one question without knowing?
How can one get lost if there was never a path?
How can one lead without wisdom?
How can one stand without strength?
How can one believe without evidence?
How can one die without life…
How can I without you… I'm incomplete

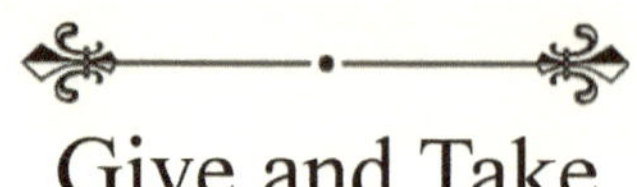

Give and Take

I give to her
Because she's generous

I work with her
Because I know she slaves for me

I write to her
Because I know she understands

I talk to her all the time
Because she listens so well

I pray for her
Because I know she won't waste the help

I wait for her
Cause I know she has patience for me

I cry for her
So, she doesn't have to

I hug her
Because she comforts me

I drive her anywhere
Because she's the best passenger

I care for her
because with all that emotion she just might care more about me
I love her
Because she perfect for me

I'll forgive her

Because I trust her

I'll trust her
Because she as honest as can be

I spent time with her
Because she's so interesting

I want her to be my kids' mother
Because I know she'll be the best

I want her to be my wife
Because I want no other

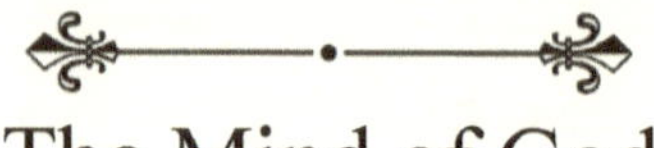

The Mind of God

Do you think God
Is envious?
That He wishes He
Were another?
OR Does He enjoy being Lord of all Creation?

Do you think God
Worries?
That he gets nervous
About a soul's wellbeing?
Or does He always have a plan without fail?

Do you think God
Feels pain
Is it possible
For the Father to hurt?
What about when His people
Are suffering… does He feel pain?
Or is He perfection without blemish?

Do you think God
Would save one
Just because He likes them so much
Even if they ain't a Christian?
Can God redeem outside the cross?
(NO)
But does He feel bad they suffer eternally?
(YES)
what is God like, His personality type?
His ways are not like our ways
For He is high above
We have to examine His Son
it's the closest we get (the express image)

He hates it when people don't believe Him
When they doubt Him
When they test Him…
He loves innocent and those who love life
He doesn't care about your past
He cares about you
He wants to help He wants to redeem
He's a people person
He meditates on His own- possibly questioning Himself- possibly wondering if any will truly get Him- possibly thinking of all the souls that will reject Him and the pain of the consequence of their actions

He isn't forcefully unless extreme circumstance_ he is very gentle and kind
He loves people that have been rejected or made mistakes or feel alone and abandoned- I believe cause they listen to Him, they receive His love
He always has a plan and knows exactly what He is doing…
He loves building up others to do His work… He doesn't wanna do everything Himself- but He helps you
He doesn't care about reigning over you- He wants to walk with you as an equal (calls you His... the Creator calls you His brother)
He doesn't despise women- He values them if they know their role
He demands a lot out of you but He equips you with everything you need
He loves talking about truth and the important things with you…

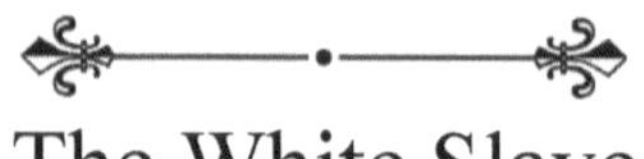

The White Slave

We worked
For them to live here
We welcomed with open arms
And they spat on us
We talked friendly
And they mocked secretly with their dialect

We preferred them with our laws
And they still broke our laws
We gave them priority over our own people
And they despised us
We opened our culture to include them
And they said we had no culture

We embraced their culture
And they blamed ours for their faults
We gave them money
And they sent it to their home country
We tried to show them love
But they only had contempt for us

We cried when one of theirs died
They applauded when they murdered ours
We tried to be one
But they wanted separation

We wanted peace
They wanted control
They were united with their people
Ours were riven in two

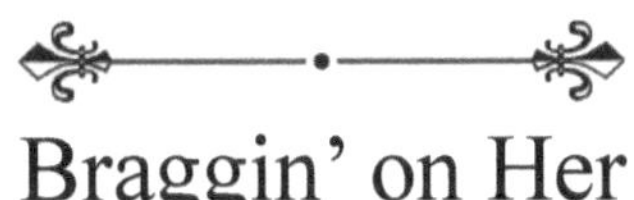

Braggin' on Her

My lover brings me pride
With all the virtues she carries out
With all the beauty of soul
That shines forth as the sun
My lover brings me joy
With her care and compassion
And the unlimited. love
That she pours on me daily
My lover brings me want
Want to do my best for her
Want to sacrifice to make her life easier
Want to be with her forever

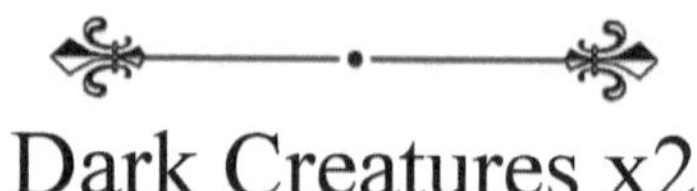

Dark Creatures x2

Loveless monsters
They come with their weapons
Raging a war with Gods people
Men cry out in despair

Selfish beasts
Protecting only themselves
They despise the righteous
Howbeit light creeps in

Arrogant creatures
They bring their torches
Showing the hatred
Yet love shines brighter

Soulless devils
Ready to burn with their enemies
Beaming darkness from their core
Thrown into a pit as dark and light separate

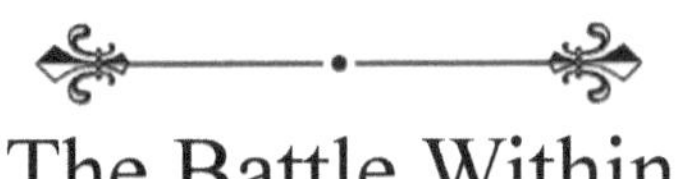

The Battle Within

I knew you...
Or so I thought...
You were so full of life
So, brim and bright with possibility
Where did I go wrong?

I trusted in you …
Thought I could rely on you
But you only let me down...
You betrayed me when I needed you most!!!
Betrayal at its darkest!

You were the voice of reason within...
The voice saying "you can do this"
But you became a naysayer...
A doubter of my success...
Will I ever escape your wrath??

That voice in my head...
Telling me I'm doomed
That feeling of despair...
Teaching me loss and pain
I've got a trump card:
GOD

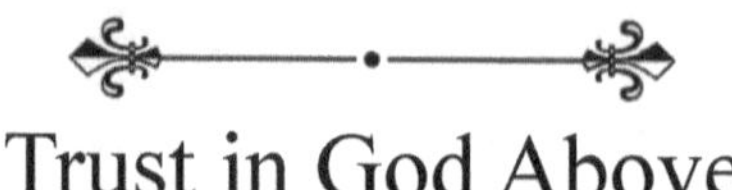

Trust in God Above

I trust
That God doesn't fail
As He is Almighty
And knows what to do
Every time everywhere and with everyone

I trust
That God answers prayers
Not too early or too late
But when the prayer means the most
And has the greatest impact

I trust
That when good suffers good is followed
For evil has no part with good
And when evil attacks good overwhelms
And prevails even in death

I trust
That my mistakes lead to good
As God redeems wrong
And makes them success
For those that put their faith in him

I trust
That when I'm hated He'll be glorified
As hating good brings shame to some
And invigorates the good
Strengthening their inner being

I trust
That God made me an equal half
Who loves God as I do

And who compliments me perfectly
Ready to suffer with me through any trial

I trust
God has more power than evil
Able to stop any wickedness
Allowing Satan to thrive now
To test His people and prove their worth

I trust
Souls last forever
Belonging to the place of peace
Or the prison of perdition
Eternally Glorying God
I'm here for you always

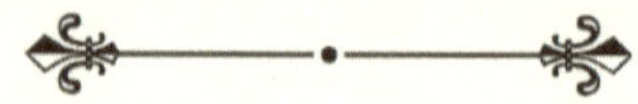

I Wasn't Myself... Forgive Me Lord

I lost my sanity...
Satan made me Gods enemy
O'er and o'er we fought...
Me against the Almighty

My vision was blurred by illness...
My hope in everything but God
I, a traitor to the cause of the cross
Hanging on to this life by a thread

I sought to replace my precious Savior
With a mere woman: a mortal
A love affair between My first Love
And one that will let me down

The confusion seeped deeply within
I obsessed over this girl
Never met her yet glorified her beyond measure...
Forgive me God!!! take me back

For she shall not save me from the wrath of God
She cannot sympathize with my pains
Or comfort me in my sorrow
Only the Almighty can reach my depths

Take my back Lord I cry!!
Never again let my love for another surpass you!!!
I plead insanity... a breakdown of despair
Lord... eternally let you be my first love from hens forth

Poor Richards nephew: Failing Serge's

Excitement tempered becomes patience; patience tempered becomes reality
Sometimes you need to lose yourself to find yourself
Love of a greater gives you something to aspire to…
Role models must model their actions and words for all to see, the best ones have grinded to the point of naturally having good actions and words
It's not conquering the world that makes you great…its conquering yourself
Without hunger, who would know to eat… without the pain of separation how would we know our love?
Music is man's answer to the birds chirping, the waterfalls flowing, and the thunderstorm quaking
Love affects everyone involved to the heart… it gives them meaning
There's void in your heart that you can't fix; seek truth until you find the answer; the reason for you here
Knowing everything is boring… discovering truth and ideas is stimulating (maybe Gods bored knowing everything I dunno… or maybe He enjoys watching us discovery)
When we don't understand we get sidetracked when we follow along, we get growth from understating
Perniciousness starts with an action that seems harmless and innocent
A life of satisfaction in the little things is a life of happiness
Torment to any human is a torment to a merciful kind soul
Who do you obey when you're free to do your own will? because you're always obeying someone whether you like it or not
Be careful who you trust; it can either support your or fail you
Sleep is one of the greatest gifts God gave us…without it life would be pain and insanity and hard to forget the times of hardship

The ones who bring the most joy can also bring you the most pain
Time seasons moon-cycles mean nothing without living beings affected by them

Laws that can be manipulated aren't laws… they enable lawlessness

When freedom is too broad anything is possible- even evil- even slavery

All life dies and leaves behind a contribution; those who willingly give their life down for a purpose leave greater seeds

One person united with truth discovers more than a million bound together by lies

One loyal loving submissive woman is worth more than all the riches in the world

Woman that understands our weaknesses as men help improve us a men

Careful who you choose; woman can make your life a living hell or heaven

Women that challenge their man intellectually yet humbly allow the man to soar to new heights

A woman worth is so much more than appearance but appearance is all we see

Woman make life worthwhile; without them life would be hell

Women who keep themselves for marriage are superior and more desirable

Woman who wanna be moms embrace womanhood; those who don't reject their gift from God

Woman who saves themselves for one man in their life are happier

True inspiration makes people better versions of themselves, not imitations of you.

The difference between fact and fiction is its harder to believe the truth

The biggest failure is when you lose hope

Peace of mind means nothing without goodness

Hardship without acknowledging your weakness results in more hardship

Pain only becomes useful after rest

Darkness begets more darkness until you reach the pivot point of light or destruction

There can't be life without hope

Struggles change you for better or worse- let them consume you and you face more struggles

Your outlook of the world and perception of self-play a big part in who you are

Control is a characteristic of the evil; servant leadership is the opposite

What good is guidance if you yourself don't know where you're going?

beauty outwardly is alluring… beauty inwardly is rewarding
Shortcomings teach us the greatest lesson… we are not God
If perfection were a virtue all other virtues would be moot and chasing them would be folly
The forlorn have the greatest success stories; better yet they can reach the most people and relate… (which is why Jesus is the perfect person to rule…. He suffered more than anyone and was tempted in everyday we are yet prevailed he was forlorn in a way by being abandoned and lonely …)
Connection to others is a type of power
It's the indefatigable that are the real winners; when you grind enough you will rise
Being well liked means little if no one's got your back
We chase others acceptance because we don't see the spiritual realm
Sometimes we want belonging to the point we lose ourselves
What good is a friend that leads you to decadence?

If you take the fall for another you better have a plan
Love is useless without another to love
Love is learned as a child before talking…, maybe because it's more important
When a man loves a woman… she can inflict more pain on him than
The rest of the world combined. please don't hurt me woman… who else will I go to
Love of self isn't love… its obsession
Love is sacrifice… if you never let go of something you can't replace it with love
Love that becomes betrayal is the most heinous of evil
Destruction of self comes you become too much or too little in your own eyes… balance is key
For every ounce of control, we have over our lives there's ten pounds worth we depend on others, and a trillion tons on God
When lies become common... no one understands each other
Open up your soul to an elite, they'll steal from you… open up your soul to a commoner they'll laugh at you… open up your soul to a true friend they'll listen… open up your soul to God and He'll heal you
You can't truly appreciate gain without first suffering loss
When seasons are bountiful our faith is tested to stay true, when seasons are dry our faith is keeps us
In the end the reward of true faith never disappoints

Heroes are those who fight and suffer for another for justices' sake… villains are those who gain and steal for controls sake

Everyman is a slave to something. if you're a slave to freedom you're a slave to Christ

It's the small choices that lead to the big moments

Fear controls. love compels

Answers often come when we quit obsessing over the question

Solitude is only conceivable with freedom

If you mind your own business… remember those in power don't

When you reject your ancestor's way… are you still considered posterity? Or have you become illegitimate?

If race didn't matter… why does racism exists?

When they start indoctrinating children… it's the beginning of the end

The difference between faith and hope is that faith expects while hope believes

Surviving day to day teaches you more than if you were set for life

Focusing on the pain makes it more intense… if you can find a distraction use it

Creativity is a superior form of intelligence

Distractions can be good or bad depending on the situation… just don't let them control you

When you obsess over something it controls you; when you're in control you can walk away anytime

Kids are the closest thing to God in the human race

Any one that hurts a child it would be better if they had. a millstone and were drowned in the bottom of the sea

Hope is powerful and hard to destroy… even death can inspire hope

Wealth of riches means nothing if you lose it all… wealth of virtue means everything even if you lose it all

When you betray a devil its redemption… when you betray a brother you become a devil

Absurdity to the logical is logic to the absurd

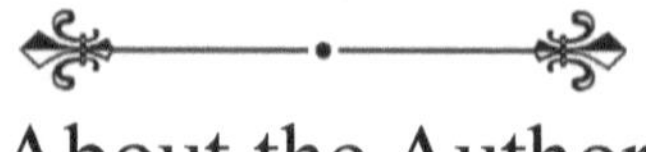

About the Author

The author is the son of a pastor and brother to 5 brothers and one sister. He grew up in multiple states growing up, including Kentucky (he roots for Big Blue) and his parents' home state where he attended high school in Minnesota (where he cheers for the pro teams, including that team that you can always count on to let you down (skol Vikings)). He is a dedicated Christian and believes strongly in Americas Christian roots and our need to return to them. He laments the decline of the American republic and prays hard for a revival or awakening or something to turn us back to the God of the forefathers. He believes that the lost causes are the only ones worth fighting for, so we should never give up on America. The city on a hill must come back or the whole world will suffer. He seeks a higher purpose in life and finds that our relations to our Creator and fellow man is the higher purpose of mankind (along with the search for truth). Sometimes, however, you just need a break from heavy thinking and do something you enjoy. For hobbies he enjoys anything a dog would: walks, car rides, great food, revisiting people I love, listening to music (punk alternative house country gospel and classical), staring at a talking television for movies (I have an extensive blu-ray collection ranging from some favorites like Its wonderful life to Lord of the Rings to Braveheart to Rudy to Back to the Future to Spiderman 2 to the marvel movies to ... I could go on for a while but yeah...I like movies), and even some things dogs can't do like games (including board (no, interesting games;) games (settlers of catan, Bloodrage, risk LOTR, Istanbul, marvel splendor, spades and dutch blitz, dominion, codenames and scatagories categories and cranium, sports like basketball, ultimate frisbee, frolf, golf, tennis, volleyball, and others (which I may not be any good at but do for love of the game) lawn games (like boccie ball, horseshoes and corn hole) and video games.